## Praise for *God's Word*

"This is not just another book about how to read the Bible. This is your invitation to a feast—to sit down at table and dine on the delectable delights of God's abundant word. The maître d' is John Kleinig, who summons you not just to analyze a complex ancient text, but to digest for yourself the rich spiritual banquet God's Spirit sets before you in holy Scripture. Kleinig's short little handbook on the Bible is itself chock full of Scripture in every sentence. I know you will come away marveling anew, as Peter did, at the words of eternal life flowing from Jesus's mouth for your ears to hear and your heart to believe."

—**Harold L. Senkbeil**, author of *The Care of Souls*

"John Kleinig knows that the word of God is not inert, as if it were up to us to make it real in our lives. In the preaching of the gospel, our Lord Jesus is doing something: he is giving us himself, together with his salvation and life and nourishment and healing and power. In case we've ever forgotten this, Kleinig reminds us of what happens to our hearts when the word of Christ gets into it and changes it from the inside out. His book is a compact celebration of what Scripture does, and it contains so much Scripture, aptly expounded and preached, that to read this book with open ears is already to experience what it is talking about."

—**Phillip Cary**, author of *Good News for Anxious Christians*; professor of philosophy, Eastern University

"A delightful invitation to the rich feast Jesus provides us in his word. It will appetize your ears, so that they might taste and see that the Lord is good!"

—**Tyler R. Wittman**, co-author of *Biblical Reasoning*; assistant professor of theology, New Orleans Baptist Theological Seminary

"Too easily, we become dusty-Bible Christians who forget that God's word is sharp, active, and alive. In *God's Word: A Guide to Holy Scripture*, Kleinig reminds us, through clear and winsome exposition, that Scripture has the power to heal, comfort, energize, and convict believers each new day. An excellent primer for all Christians about the Bible as a whole."

—**Rachel Joy Welcher**, author of *Talking Back to Purity Culture*

# GOD'S WORD

**See also these titles in the
Christian Essentials Series**

*The Ten Commandments*
by Peter J. Leithart

*The Apostles' Creed*
by Ben Myers

*The Lord's Prayer*
by Wesley Hill

*Baptism*
by Peter J. Leithart

# GOD'S WORD

A Guide to Holy Scripture

## JOHN W. KLEINIG

LEXHAM PRESS

*God's Word: A Guide to Holy Scripture*
Christian Essentials

Copyright 2022 John W. Kleinig

Lexham Press, 1313 Commercial St., Bellingham, WA 98225
LexhamPress.com

Print ISBN 9781683596431
Digital ISBN 9781683596448
Library of Congress Number 2022937657

Lexham Editorial: Todd Hains, Jeff Reimer, Katie French, Kelsey Matthews, Mandi Newell
Cover Design: Brittany Schrock
Typesetting: Abigail Stocker, Justin Marr

*To my parents Ben (1901–1985) and Frieda Kleinig (1907–2000)*
*who nourished me from infancy with the gospel of Christ*
*at home and in church, and my Lutheran ancestors*
*on both sides of my family who migrated to*
*Australia from Prussia to escape*
*religious discrimination and*
*persecution for their*
*faithfulness to*
*God's word*

# CONTENTS

# CHRISTIAN ESSENTIALS

# SERIES PREFACE

T he Christian Essentials series passes down tradition that matters.

The church has often spoken paradoxically about growth in Christian faith: to grow means to stay at the beginning. The great Reformer Martin Luther exemplified this. "Although I'm indeed an old doctor," he said, "I never move on from the childish doctrine of the Ten Commandments and the Apostles' Creed and the Lord's Prayer. I still daily learn and pray them with my little Hans and my little Lena." He had just as much to learn about the Lord as his children.

The ancient church was founded on basic biblical teachings and practices like the Ten Commandments, baptism, the Apostles' Creed, the Lord's Supper, the Lord's Prayer, and corporate worship. These basics of the Christian life have sustained and nurtured every generation of the faithful—from the apostles to today. They apply equally to old and young, men and women, pastors and church members. "In Christ Jesus you are all sons of God through faith" (Gal 3:26).

We need the wisdom of the communion of saints. They broaden our perspective beyond our current culture and time. "Every age has its own outlook," C. S. Lewis wrote. "It is specially good at seeing certain truths and specially liable to make certain mistakes." By focusing on what's current, we rob ourselves of the insights and questions of those who have gone before us. On the other hand, by reading our forebears in faith, we engage ideas that otherwise might never occur to us.

The books in the Christian Essentials series open up the meaning of the foundations of our faith. These basics are unfolded afresh for today in conversation with the great tradition—grounded in and strengthened by Scripture—for the continuing growth of all the children of God.

> *Hear, O Israel: The Lord our God, the Lord is one. You shall love the Lord your God with all your heart and with all your soul and with all your might. And these words that I command you today shall be on your heart. You shall teach them diligently to your children, and shall talk of them when you sit in your house, and when you walk by the way, and when you lie down, and when you rise. You shall bind them as a sign on your hand, and they shall be as frontlets between your eyes. You shall write them on the doorposts of your house and on your gates. (Deut 6:4–9)*

# PRAYER FOR HEARING GOD'S WORD

**T**his order of prayer invites you to read each chapter in the book as a devotional exercise by yourself. It can also be used by a group—with a leader speaking the plain text and the group speaking the words in bold.

## IN GOD'S NAME

In the name of the Father and the Son and the Holy Spirit.
**Amen.**

O Lord, open my lips
**and my mouth will declare your praise.**     *Psalm 51:15*
Make haste, O God, to deliver me
**make haste to help me, O Lord.**     *Psalm 70:1*
Teach me to do your will, for you are my God
**Let your good Spirit lead me on a level path.**     *Psalm 143:10*

**Glory be to the Father and the Son and the Holy Spirit:**
**as it was in the beginning, is now, and will be forever. Amen.**

## THE PROMISES OF JESUS

Jesus says, "Blessed are those who hear the word of God and keep it." *Luke 11:28*

Jesus also says, "When the Spirit of truth comes, he will guide you into all the truth, for he will not speak on his own, but will speak whatever he hears. He will glorify me, because he will take what is mine and declare it to you." *John 16:13–14*

## RESPONSIVE PRAYER

Lord, your word is a lamp to my feet
**and a light to my path.** *Psalm 119:105*
Your promises have been thoroughly tested,
**and your servant loves them.** *v. 140*
How sweet are your words to my taste,
**sweeter than honey to my mouth!** *v. 103*
I rise before dawn and cry for help;
**I hope in your words.** *v. 147*
My eyes are awake before each watch of the night,
**that I may meditate on your promise.** *v. 148*
I entreat your favor with all my heart;
**be gracious to me according to your promise.** *v. 58*
Let my plea come before you;
**deliver me according to your promise.** *v. 170*
I am severely afflicted
**give me life, O Lord, according to your word!** *v. 107*
Let your steadfast love comfort me

**according to your promise to your servant.** *v. 76*

Let my cry come before you, O Lord

**give me understanding according to your word.** *v. 169*

Direct my footsteps according to your word,

**let no sin rule over me.** *v. 133*

I rejoice in your word

**like one who finds great treasure.** *v. 162*

Oh, how I love your law!

**I meditate on it all day long.** *v. 97*

My tongue will sing of your word,

**for all your commandments are right.** *v. 172*

The Lord is my portion;

**I promise to keep your words.** *v. 57*

Your word is a lamp to my feet

**and a light to my path.** *v. 105*

# CLOSING PRAYER

Blessed Lord, you have caused all holy Scriptures to be written for our learning. Grant that we may so hear them, read, mark, learn, and inwardly digest them that, by patience and comfort of your holy word, we may embrace and ever hold fast the blessed hope of everlasting life; through Jesus Christ, our Lord. **Amen.**

This is my only comfort in my trouble,

**for your word has given me life.** *Psalm 119:50 BCP*

Let us bless the Lord.

**Thanks be to God.**

# I

# AN INVITATION TO A BANQUET

Blessed is anyone who will eat
bread in the kingdom of God.
*Luke 14:15 NRSV*

This is a little book about a big book, not any book, but God's book. More correctly, it is a book about God's word, his speech that comes to us in a written, spoken, and embodied form. I do not intend to set out an argument to prove anything about the Bible as God's written word, let alone explain its divine nature and inspiration. That would be like trying to prove the value of good food. You can only really discover how tasty and nourishing and satisfying food is by eating it. Its value is shown by its effect on you. This book is much more like an extended invitation for you to enjoy a lavish meal with many different dishes by getting you to sample some of it, an unusual banquet in which you can feast

1

on God's words by listening to them and mulling over them to digest and assimilate them, a heavenly meal in which you are nourished by God's Holy Spirit.

This meal is the festive banquet that God himself foretold by a prophecy about the coming Messiah in Isaiah 55:1–9. It is a rich banquet that God himself promised to provide, a free meal that would truly satisfy, a supernatural feast that would be enjoyed by "eating" with the ears rather than the mouth. As had been prophesied in Isaiah 25:6–9, that meal celebrates the death of death. In Isaiah 55:1–3 God himself invites people to it with these words:

> Come, everyone who thirsts, come to the waters;
>> and he who has no money, come, buy and eat.
> Come, buy wine and milk
>> without money and without price.
> Why do you spend your money
>> for that which is not bread,
>> and your labor for what does not satisfy?
> Listen intently to me, and eat what is good,
>> and delight yourselves with rich food.
> Incline your ear, and come to me;
>> hear that your soul may live.

This banquet is hosted by the Messiah, the royal successor and heir of David. He spreads a heavenly feast for people here on earth. In it guests from all nations benefit from God's covenant with David together with God's people. In it they, rather strangely, feast on his life-giving word. Pardoned by God, they share in the status, resources, and mission of God's royal Son.

What God promised in this prophecy was fulfilled by the life, death, and resurrection of Jesus Christ. He was sent by God the Father to host a heavenly meal on earth for people from all nations. That includes you and me. He who alone can teach you heavenly wisdom for your life on earth now issues this invitation to you:

Come, eat of my bread
    and drink the wine that I have mixed.
Lay aside immaturity, and live,
    and walk in the way of insight. (Prov 9:5–6)

He invites you to participate in that meal and enjoy its inexhaustible spread. If you accept that invitation and listen to him, you will join those guests of Jesus, who "have tasted the heavenly gift, and shared in the Holy Spirit, and have tasted the goodness of the word of God and the powers of the age to come" (Heb 6:4–5). Even if you have not yet joined that celebration, this invitation is for you too and all people.

Since this book is meant to invite you to participate in the heavenly feast that consists of God's words to you and all people, I do not want you to merely read what I write about them; I urge you to listen attentively to his words for yourselves, meditate on them, and enjoy the goodness that they offer. Otherwise you will be like people who watch a cooking show on television but do not have the satisfaction and enjoyment that they could have if they cooked and ate the food that was shown to them. Such a virtual meal may help to reduce weight, but it does not provide any nourishment.

Here is the menu of this real, spiritually nourishing meal for you! The Triune God uses his written word in the Bible to feed you with supernatural food, like the gift of manna to the Israelites in the desert. In that book the Triune God—Father, Son, and Holy Spirit—speaks with one voice to deliver heavenly gifts to people on earth. Through authoritative speech that is powerful and performative, God does something great for them and for you. God the Father offers and delivers Jesus as a benefactor to those who listen to him. Through the gospel of Jesus, its hearers receive the Holy Spirit and his spiritual blessings, such as salvation and life, nourishment and healing, deliverance and empowerment. As with a smorgasbord, there are many courses that are part of a lavish meal. There is much more on the menu than can be enjoyed in any single sitting, food enough for a lifetime. Even though it is a communal meal that is best enjoyed communally with other guests in a communal assembly, much of it can also be received devotionally in a family gathering or individually as you read this little book.

So welcome to a heavenly meal, a meal of plain words, a rich feast that alone can satisfy you fully. And listen, intently and wholeheartedly, to what God says to you and receive what God offers you dish by dish as you are ready to enjoy each course of the meal. Join the feast! Check out for yourself the

Bible passages that I mention, like the Jews in Berea (Acts 17:11); "taste and see that the LORD is good" (Ps 34:8). Enjoy the meal!

**BLESSED LORD,** you have caused all holy Scriptures to be written for our learning.

Grant that we may so hear them,

read, mark, learn, and inwardly digest them

that, by patience and comfort of your

holy Word,

we may embrace and ever hold fast the

blessed hope of everlasting life;

through Jesus Christ, our Lord.

**AMEN.**

# II

# THE GOD WHO SPEAKS

Heaven and earth will pass away, but
my words will never pass away.

*Luke 21:33 ESV*

**W**e have a God who speaks. God the Father speaks, God the Son speaks, and God the Holy Spirit speaks. God did not just speak long ago and then become silent. As he spoke then, so he still speaks now. Thus the author of Hebrews surprises us by quoting passages from the Old Testament in which the congregation that he addresses hears the Father speaking (Heb 1:5–13; 5:6; 12:26), the Son speaking (2:12–13; 10:5–7), and the Holy Spirit speaking (3:7–11; 10:15–17). Even though they each speak with their own voices, they do not speak separately but together with each other in a coherent, eternal conversation. They all have the same message because they all speak about Jesus. Both the Father and the

Spirit bear witness to Jesus, just as he bears witness to himself (John 5:36–38; 8:18; 15:26). Both the prophetic authors of the Old Testament and the apostolic authors of the New Testament also bear witness to Jesus (John 5:39; 15:27; Luke 24:28). All this makes up a single conversation of the Triune God with his people and them with him and each other. Since we have a record of that conversation in the Bible, we can listen in on it and join in with it. There is room in it for us all—both as hearers and speakers.

In a written sermon for his congregation, the author of Hebrews sums up the main features of God's spoken word simply and yet profoundly: "In the past God spoke to our forefathers through the prophets at many times and in various ways, but in these last days he has spoken to us by his Son, whom he appointed heir of all things, and through whom he made the universe. The Son is the radiance of God's glory and the exact representation of his being, sustaining all things by his powerful word" (1:1–3 NIV84). What surprises me about this eloquent summary is its assertion that the same God who spoke to our spiritual ancestors first through the prophets and then by his Son also now speaks to us as members of the same community when we gather in worship. There the God who spoke to his people at Mt. Sinai speaks to us now (Heb 12:22–25).

I t is obvious to any reader that the Bible contains many words about God. Some of these are marked as words that God speaks; others are the words of the people who report them.

So it comes as a surprise to discover that all the many words of God are regarded as a single word, a single speech with a single message by Jesus and the apostles. Take, for example, the book of Acts. There Luke refers summarily to all that the prophets and apostles taught as "the word" (twelve times in all), or "God's word" (ten times in all), or "the word of the Lord" (nine times in all). Taken together, both the Old Testament and the New Testament speak a single word: the word of salvation (Acts 13:26), the word of grace (Acts 14:3), the word of the gospel (Acts 15:7). So, somewhat audaciously, the Bible is held to report the speech of the one and only God. Just as he is one, so his word is one.

T he story of God's speech in the Bible begins with God's creation of the universe and the earth as a home for the human family. He calls it into existence and sustains it with his creative speech (Heb 1:3; 11:3). He speaks the world into being by what he decrees and upholds it with the same powerful word that created it (Ps 33:8–9; 148:8–9). Thus if he would no longer say, "Let there be light," there would no more be any light (Gen 1:3). If he no longer told the earth to produce vegetation and animate creatures, all life would cease to exist on earth (Gen 1:11, 24). God the Father creates the world through his Son (John 1:3, 10; Col 1:16). The Son is both God's agent in creation and the heir who inherits it from him (Col 1:16).

Just as a play enacts the word of its author and producer, so the story of the world is an enactment of God's word with God the Father as its author and the Son as its producer. Psalm 33:6 takes this one step further: "By the word of the Lord the heavens were made, and all their host by the breath of his mouth." Here the word that is translated by "breath" is also the Hebrew word for God's Spirit. Just as we use our breath to speak words, so God employs his Spirit to speak his word. The Spirit of God that hovered over the chaotic waters (Gen 1:2) is the creative power that is at work in and through God's word. His Spirit not only creates and upholds the order of the cosmos but also creates and sustains all life on earth (Ps 104:30; Job 33:4). Thus God creates the world by his word and his Holy Spirit.

The first part of the Bible, the Old Testament, records how the same God who spoke the world into being spoke also his word to the people of Israel (Ps 147:19–20). He spoke to them through a long line of prophets beginning with Noah and ending with Malachi. The prophets were his spokesmen who were sent to speak his word to his people. Through them God translates what he wants to say into human language. God puts his words into their mouth and tells them what they should say (Deut 18:18; 1 Kgs 17:24). They speak in his name (Deut 18:19; Jas 5:10). So they usually introduce their message by saying, "Thus says the LORD" or "Hear the word of the LORD" or some such formula.

Inspired as they are by God's Spirit (Isa 48:16; 2 Tim 3:16; 2 Pet 1:21), they are filled with divine power to speak his word (Mic 3:18). Through them God sends his words to his people by his Holy Spirit (Zech 7:12). As messengers of God, they, like Jeremiah, speak powerful words that shape the history and destiny of Israel and the nations (Jer 1:9–10). They speak many different words that do different things in different circumstances. They speak covenant words by which God commits himself to Noah's descendants and the patriarchs, to Israel and to David, and claim their commitment to him; they speak words of institution by which God authorizes, establishes, and sanctifies the tabernacle as his dwelling place, the priesthood, the divine service, and Israel as a liturgical community; they speak life-giving ordinances by which his people receive blessings from him in the promised land; they, most commonly, speak prophetic oracles by which God either saves his people from disaster or passes judgment on them for their infidelity. These oracles do not just foretell what God will do, but actually enact his word. Since they accomplish what they say, a mark of a true prophet is that what they say happens (Deut 18:21–22).

So from the call of Abram to the announcement of the Messiah by John the Baptist, God shapes his people by speaking with them. They are a unique nation who had God's word spoken to them (Ps 147:19–20). Their life as a nation was shaped for better or worse by whether they listened to God's word or whether they refused to listen to it. They therefore became a people of the book, God's book. And their basic confession of faith begins with a summons to listen: "Hear, O Israel: The LORD is our God, the LORD is one" (Deut 6:4).

The second part of the Bible, the New Testament, records how God's speaking through the prophets culminates in his speaking to us by his Son (Heb 1:2). It is as if the producer of a play stepped on stage as the main actor in it. He ushered in the goal of human history by his incarnation as a man. By his Son, God the Father spoke to people not just in human words but also in the idiom of a human life. He spoke as much by who he was, what he did, and what he was like, as by what he said. He did not just represent God the Father but was the exact representation of his being (Heb 1:3). By his life, death, and resurrection as a human being, he rescued the human family from destruction and reclaimed it for himself and his Father. He accomplished that by speaking and enacting his Father's word; for through the words of Jesus, the Father who dwells in him performed his work of salvation (John 14:10).

This is so because his words are the words of the Father who sent him (John 14:24). He does not speak his own word by his own authority but the word of the Father who sent him (John 12:49). He declares what he has heard from the Father (8:26; 15:15) and tells what the Father teaches him to say (8:28). And not just long ago to his apostles but also to us now. Through the word that Jesus speaks, the Father speaks to us.

What's more, the Holy Spirit also speaks to us through his word (John 16:12–15). He takes the words of Jesus and applies them to us who live this side of Christ's death and resurrection, so that they speak to us personally and work for us. The Holy Spirit reminds us that what Jesus said and did in his earthly ministry shows us what he is saying and doing for us now in the church. Through the Spirit the word of Jesus dwells in us and has its proper effect on us.

We benefit from a supernatural chain of transmission that reaches down from heaven to earth and comes down through time to us. Through that chain of speakers and writers, God's word comes to us and reaches us here and now. God's word is handed down from him to us. It is given in order to be received in faith and kept by those who hear it (John 17:5–6). By keeping it, they receive what it gives (John 8:51–52). The Father gives his word to his Son, who keeps it (John 8:55). He, in turn, gives it to his apostles (John 17:8, 14), who keep it (John 17:6). His apostles, then, hand his word on to others by their proclamation of it (John 17:20), so that they too can receive it and its gifts by keeping it (John 14:23); if they keep his word by retaining it, God the Father and Jesus will come to love them and make their home with them.

At this point, the picture changes from the retention of the word to the inhabitation of it. The word of Jesus provides his disciples with a place to be. Earlier in John's Gospel, Jesus had said this to those who believed in him, "If you abide in my word, you are truly my disciples, and you will know the truth, and the truth will set you free" (John 8:31–32). Those who do not just visit his word occasionally but stay within it and inhabit it will be taught the truth about themselves and God, the truth that sets them free from all spiritual danger and uncertainty about God. It will be a safe place for them, a place of truth and freedom. By abiding in his word, which abides in them (John 5:38; 15:7), they will abide in Jesus as a safe place (15:4, 5, 7) and have Jesus abiding in them (15:4). Best of all, like children with their loving parents and a wife with her loving husband, they will abide in his love just as Jesus abides in his Father's love (John 15:10). They will be with Jesus in the holy place where he is with the Father (John 17:24; cf. 7:34, 36; 8:22; 12:26). His word will provide them with a place to be, a place of freedom and love, a place to flourish and be fruitful, a place of honor and glory, a foyer of heaven on earth.

Because God's word is eternal, it provides a secure place to be in an ever-changing world.

Even though it is spoken in time, it transcends all time and offers God's gifts to people at all times and in all places. Psalm 119:89–90 rightly acknowledges that it is eternal because it is fixed in the heavens. Through his eternal word, God maintains his order on earth and shows his faithfulness to all generations. Thus God not only promised that his prophetic word would remain forever (Isa 40:8) but also now fulfills that promise through the imperishable gospel of Jesus (1 Pet 1:23–25). The gospel is "the living and abiding word of God" that remains when everything else perishes, the word that stands forever. Since it stands forever, it gives us the place where we can stand with God forever. Jesus therefore solemnly declares that even though heaven and earth will eventually cease to be, his words will never pass away (Luke 21:33). They will remain in force for all time and for eternity.

# BLESSED LORD

# III

# WORDS THAT DO WHAT THEY SAY

He spoke, and it was done.

*Psalm 33:9 KJV*

I n Isaiah 55:10–11, God himself has this to say about the power of his prophetic word, the promise of salvation that he spoke to his people through Isaiah:

For as the rain and the snow come down from heaven
    and do not return there but water the earth,
making it bring forth and sprout,
    giving seed to the sower and bread for the eater,
so shall my word be that goes out of my mouth;
    it shall not return to me empty,
but shall accomplish that which I purpose,
    and shall succeed in the thing for which I sent it.

Whether it is spoken by the prophet Isaiah or by the whole Bible, God's word is like the rain and snow that water the earth and produce life in it. It is powerful and performative, effective and productive.

That is also true in some measure for human speech. Its power is evident and apparent to any discerning observer of human affairs. For better or worse, words shape the history of the world and our lives in all their parts. Constructive speech produces good results that benefit us all; destructive speech does great damage to all life on earth. Constructive speech promotes prosperity and peace; destructive speech unleashes conflict and chaos. Thus James rightly notes a tongue that was set alight by hell has the power to set on fire the whole course of life on earth (3:6). It has the power to spread diabolical disorder and promote divine harmony (3:13–18).

The power of human speech is shown by the way that language works and how we use it. We use descriptive speech honestly to say how things really are, or dishonestly to falsify what is really so. We use imperative speech morally to get others to do what is right, or immorally to urge them to do what is wrong. Most significantly, we use performative speech beneficially to achieve something good, like declaring peace, or detrimentally to do something evil, like declaring an unjust war. Yet, despite its obvious power, the effect of human speech is limited by the limitations of the speaker. It cannot create anything. It seldom achieves all that it sets out to do, and then only for a short while, if at all. It is all too often empty speech.

Isaiah notes that God's speech differs from human speech in two ways. On the one hand, unlike human speech, it only does what is good. Even when it is spoken in judgment, God's word judges sin in order to pardon sinners (Isa 55:6–9). On the other hand, it always accomplishes what God wants. It does what it says; it delivers what it promises to give; it achieves its purpose; it is always effective. Just as the rain and snow that water the earth germinate the seeds of wheat that are sown in it, nourish the plants that shoot up from the ground, and provide a harvest of grain for human farmers, so God's word is productive. It generates new life, nourishes it so that it grows and flourishes, and produces a good harvest of grain with flour and bread for people to eat. So then, God's word that is spoken to people on earth is like his powerful word that creates and sustains the world and life in it; it does what it says.

We can see this best in the stories of Jesus in the four Gospels. When they report what Jesus does, they, in most cases, show that Jesus accomplishes this by what he says. This happens in many different ways in different circumstances with different people. Take, for example, Mark's Gospel. Jesus calls his first four disciples by saying, "Follow me and I will make you become fishers of men" (1:17; 2:14). He silences an unclean spirit and drives it from a man by saying, "Be silent, and come out of him!" (1:25). He heals a leper by saying, "Be clean" (1:42). He forgives a crippled man by saying, "Son, your sins are forgiven" (2:5) and heals him by saying, "Rise, pick up your bed, and go home" (2:11). He heals a man with a withered hand by saying, "Stretch out your hand" (3:5). He calms the storm on a lake by saying, "Be still!" (4:39). He dispatches many demons from a man by saying, "Come out of the man, you unclean spirit!" (5:8). He heals a woman with an irregular menstrual discharge by saying, "Daughter, your faith has made you well; go in peace, and be healed of your disease" (5:34). He revives a dead girl by saying, "Little girl, I say to you, arise" (5:41). He comforts his terrified disciples facing the prospect of drowning in a storm on the lake by saying, "Take heart; it is I. Do not be afraid" (6:50). He drives a demon from the daughter of a gentile woman by saying, "The demon has left your daughter" (7:29). He gives hearing and speech to a deaf-mute man by saying, "Be opened" (7:34). He heals a demon-possessed boy by saying, "You mute and deaf spirit, I command you, come out of him and never enter him again" (9:25). He restores the sight of a blind beggar by saying, "Go your way; your faith has made you well" (10:52). He withers a fruitless fig tree by saying, "Let no one eat fruit from you ever again" (11:14 NKJV). Most amazingly, in his final Passover meal with his disciples, Jesus gives bread and wine to his disciples as his body and blood by saying, "Take; this is my body; ... this is my blood of the new covenant, which is poured out for many" (14:24).

These words of Jesus are performative utterances that accomplish what he says. Some are declarations that do not tell what has happened but actually make it happen (Mark 2:5; 7:29;

10:54; 14:24). But most of them are decrees that do not just command what must be done but actually accomplish what they command. They give what they command. The most surprising of these commands are passive decrees that announce what God is accomplishing and giving by what Jesus says. Thus he tells a leper to be cleansed in 1:41 and a woman to be healed in 5:34.

Jesus does not just do what he says with these utterances, but he does his Father's work more generally by his teaching. In his teaching he always sets out to accomplish something quite specific by what he says with those whom he instructs. He teaches with authority (Luke 4:31–32). Take, for example, a number of cases in Mark's Gospel. In 2:16–17 he passes judgment on his critics who attack him for eating and drinking with sinners and accepts the tax collector Levi and others like him as his disciples. In 4:1–34 he uses parables to initiate his disciples into the mystery of his identity as the Messiah who ushers in God's kingdom by his proclamation, and to commission them to bring it to others by teaching them God's word. In 8:31–9:1 he foretells his own suffering, death, and resurrection in order to call his disciples to travel with him in the way of salvation. In 13:1–37 he urges his disciples to stay awake spiritually by teaching them about the end of the world. In every case he tells them what he is doing and shows them how they fit in with what he is doing. By teaching them, he equips them to be his disciples and authorizes them to join him in his mission to the world.

The author of Hebrews describes the power of God's word most memorably in 4:12: "The word of God is living and active, sharper than any two-edged sword (knife), piercing to the division of soul and spirit, of joints and marrow, and discerning the thoughts and intentions of the heart." He emphasizes its four main activities. First, since it is the living word of the living God, it gives and sustains life. It does not just enhance our natural, human vitality but enables us to participate in God's vitality, his eternal life. Second, it is active and effective. It is at work in us. It energizes us and enables us to do what God calls us to do, what we would not have the capacity to accomplish unless God himself empowered us. Third, like the use of a scalpel in open-heart surgery, it cuts deep inside us to remove the infection in us and heal us. It penetrates our bodies and souls and fixes up what is wrong with us. Fourth, it is able to do this because it is critical and insightful. Like an x-ray or a sonar scan, it sees what is hidden from human sight and discerns the secrets of hearts. It is therefore able to diagnose their maladies and provide the right treatment for them. So God's living word passes through our ears into our hearts and touches our conscience. There it does its hidden work in us. There we receive what it offers to us and gives us. There we experience its life-giving, healing power. It has the power to save us.

Yet, even though God's word accomplishes what God intends to achieve with it, it does not do so automatically. It is not always obviously successful, because it only delivers God's gifts to those who depend on it to receive them. Jesus himself teaches this in the parable of the seed and the soil (Matt 13:1–23; Mark 4:1–20; Luke 8:4–15). He explains that the word he teaches sometimes fails to reach its goal because its proper effect depends as much on the receptive disposition of its hearers as on its divine power. Its operation is sabotaged by three kinds of hearing—the unreceptive hearing of those who let the devil snatch the word from their hearts before it can produce saving faith and an understanding of what it has to give; the shallow hearing of those who receive the word that produces faith for a while and then abandon it in hard times; the distracted hearing of those who hear the word but let other things that demand their immediate attention choke it out in their hearts, so that it does not bear fruit.

In contrast to these three unproductive, unfruitful kinds of hearing, the right kind of hearing is productive and fruitful. Yet that is not completely true; God's word makes them productive and fruitful. It produces a bumper crop and rich harvest in those who do not just hear what it says but hear it with an understanding of what it provides (Matt 13:23), those who receive it with wholehearted acceptance (Mark 4:20) and retain it permanently in their hearts (Luke 8:15). As they receive God's word and what it offers them, they become fruitful and remain fruitful. Jesus has this to say about the one who has his word: "to him who has more, more will be given, and he will have in abundance" (Matt 13:12). Through his word, God lavishes his gifts on its faithful hearers because they have ears that hear and eyes that see (Matt 13:16–17). They are truly blessed because they keep on receiving what God conveys to them in his word; they receive more and more gifts from him (Matt 13:11–12; Luke 8:18). In Mark, Jesus adds another factor to their reception of God's gifts: "Pay attention to what you hear: with the measure you use, it will be measured to you, and still more will be added to you" (4:24). The more the disciples listen to God's word, the more they will receive from God through it; and the more they receive from God through his word, the greater will be their capacity to receive his gifts (Mark 4:24–25). Faithful hearing enhances receptivity and results in ever-increasing reception.

Because God's word does what it says and delivers what it promises, it is the word of truth (John 17:17). It is reliable and trustworthy because God is faithful and true (1 Cor 10:8; 2 Cor 1:18; 1 Thess 5:24). He is the true God who is right in his judgments (Ps 119:137, 142; John 8:16, 26) and faithful in keeping his promises (Heb 10:23). What's more, his Son Jesus is also the true God who brings us grace and truth from his Father and is himself the truth (1 John 5:20; see also John 1:14, 17; 14:6). By his law with its commandments and warnings, God truly shows us what is right and what is wrong; he truly discloses our sin (Rom 3:20) and truly guides us in the way of truth (Ps 86:11), so that we may know his will for us and do what pleases him (1 John 3:23). By his gospel, the word of truth for our salvation, God regenerates us and conveys Christ and all his blessings to us (Eph 1:13; Col 1:5–6; Jas 1:16–18). So the proof of God's words comes from our reliance on them for our salvation and protection from spiritual attack (Ps 12:5–6). By our experience of its power, we discover for ourselves that God's words are true (Ps 119:40; Prov 30:5). They are tested by their impact and effect on us. By our dependence on them, we discover that God truly does what he says. We come to know the truth that sets us free (John 8:32).

# IV

# HEARING EARS

Blessed are your eyes, for they see,
and your ears, for they hear.

*Matthew 13:16 ESV*

The first sermon that I ever preached as a seminary student was on Mark 7:31–37, a text assigned to me by my professor. I was so puzzled by it that I had to work hard to understand what happened in this story and even harder to discover what to preach from it. Little did I realize then how much that story would eventually shape my thinking about the function of the Gospels, God's word, and the whole Bible. The stimulus for my approach was the only word that Jesus speaks in this story, the Aramaic word *ephphatha,* which means "Be opened!" That word brought about a radical shift in my thinking: Instead of asking what the stories about Jesus in the Gospels *meant,* I asked what Jesus *did* in them.

This remarkable story of a deaf-mute man is full of puzzling oddities. He does not come to Jesus, but he is brought to him by others who beg Jesus to lay his hand on him. Yet Jesus does not do that. Instead, he puts his fingers into the unhearing ears of the man, puts some spittle on his tied tongue, looks up to the sky, sighs like a person in pain, and says, "Be opened!" By means of this word, which the tongue-tied man could not even hear, a word that was not addressed to him but to his ears and tongue, the man receives the ability to hear and the power of unimpeded speech that enables him to speak properly. And all that immediately! What happens is not just a series of separate acts but a single enactment in which the word of Jesus is accompanied by four acts that serve as visible, telling signs that culminate in what Jesus says. Mark highlights that word by giving it in Aramaic, because it was, most likely, already then familiar to his Roman audience as part of their rite for baptism, which we now know from the later record of its use in Rome.

For me the most puzzling feature of this account is the grammatical form of *ephphatha*. It is a passive imperative, which is used here and elsewhere to make a pronouncement that is fulfilled by God as it is spoken by Jesus. Thus when Jesus says to the leper in Mark 1:41, "Be cleansed!" he is healed immediately. When Jesus says, "Be silenced," an unclean spirit and a raging storm fall silent (Mark 1:25; 4:39). When Jesus says, "Be healed," a woman becomes well again (5:34). Just so in Mark 7:34! Here Jesus does not tell the man to open his ears and his tongue. Instead, Jesus does this for him by speaking this word.

This performative pronouncement of Jesus gives what it commands. It gives the gift of hearing and speech. It creates hearing ears and a speaking tongue. The fact that Jesus lifts up his eyes to the sky shows that it is God who opens the man's ears and eyes through what Jesus says. This effective decree is much like the creative words that God spoke to create and maintain an ordered world in the first chapter of Genesis. It could well be paraphrased by saying, "Be opened by God!" This word gives what it says because Jesus speaks it with divine authority as the agent and spokesman of his heavenly Father.

The deaf-mute man does nothing to free himself from his predicament. In fact, he even needs to be brought to Jesus by his friends. He simply receives the gift of hearing and speech from God as it is delivered to him by the word that Jesus speaks. The result is that he thereby becomes an active agent who hears Jesus and speaks properly to Jesus and other people. He is a re-created person. The onlookers understand that this is so. They recognize that God has done this and appreciate its significance. In astonishment they echo what is written in Genesis 1 about God's good work as the Creator of the universe by saying, "He has done all things well" (Mark 7:37).

I n retrospect, I now see how this story set me on a long journey of discovery. It did not provide me with some important keys to discover the meaning of the Bible. The art of interpretation supplied those for me. Instead, this story gave me insight into the function and use of the Gospels as God's word.

It showed me that the four Gospels, and in fact the whole of the Bible, bear explicit and implicit witness not just to what Jesus said and did two thousand years ago before his death and resurrection but also to what Jesus says and does now. He is "the same yesterday and today and forever" (Heb 13:8).

This story also alerted me to the power of God's word as divine performative speech. Since it was God's word, it did what it said. It did not just communicate information about divine matters, but actually provided divine help in many different ways. The gospel of Jesus actually delivered him and all his gifts to those who trusted in it and attended to it. By receiving the divine word as it addressed them, they heard the voice of the living God.

That story also showed me that the creative power of God's word does what human words cannot do. When we speak we address people who have not only physical ears that hear the sound of our words but also the mental capacity to hear what they say. But when Jesus speaks to unbelievers, he addresses people who have no capacity to hear and understand what he is saying. Although they are able to hear human speech, they are deaf to God's voice even when he speaks to them with human speech. They hear a human voice with their human ears but do not hear him. They are spiritually deaf and blind. Since their ears are not attuned to him, they do not see what he offers them. So Jesus breaks through the barrier of deaf unbelief by speaking his word to them with divine authority, a word that creates the faith that hears it and receives what it gives, a word that gives hearing and transforms spiritually deaf people into hearers and speakers, so that they can join in the great, supernatural conversation that is initiated and led by the Triune God. They do not just initially depend on the word of Jesus to become hearers but remain dependent on it to remain hearers, with ears that hear what he says and eyes that see what he is saying. Only if they remain in his word (John 8:31) and his word remains in them (John 15:7; 1 John 2:14, 24) can they continue to be his disciples. They need to keep his word so that it can exert its power in them and deliver its benefits to them continually (John 8:51–52; 14:23; 17:6; 1 John 2:5; Rev 3:8). They depend on him and his word for everything. Apart from it they possess nothing spiritually and are not able to do anything spiritually (John 15:5).

An even more amazing instance of the creative power of Christ's word is recorded in Luke 7:11–17. This story tells how Jesus resuscitated the dead son of a widow in Nain. Since he was dead, he had not just lost his sense of hearing but all his senses. Yet when Jesus addresses him personally and says, "Young man, I say to you, arise," he hears those words. This address with its command is so powerful that it restores life and hearing and speech to him. That restoration is so, too, for all Christians who, like that young man, were once spiritually dead and yet have been raised to life by Jesus (Eph 2:1–7; 5:14).

There is something of a mystery in our ability to hear spoken language and, even more so, our capacity to hear and understand God's speech. Even though we, unless we are born deaf, are born with the ability to hear the sound of human speech; we are not born with the capacity to understand a particular language. That kind of hearing is an acquired ability. It comes from living in a social context where that language is spoken. Thus my exposure to spoken English has produced my ability to hear it with understanding and speak it intelligibly. The more I hear it spoken, the more I am able to hear what is said. So, in that sense language itself creates the ability to hear it.

This is even more so with God's speech. We hear it first as nothing but human speech. To hear it as God's speech, a different kind of hearing is needed, the hearing of faith (Gal 3:2, 5). Like human speech, the ability to hear it with understanding, instead of an incomprehensible foreign language, comes from our exposure to it. The work of the Holy Spirit through his word creates the capacity to hear his voice and understand what he says (1 Cor 2:12). God himself gives that ability through his word.

That gift of hearing is mentioned in both parts of the Bible. Thus in Deuteronomy 29:4, Moses laments, "To this day the LORD has not given you a heart to understand or eyes to see or ears to hear." That had come about by their refusal to receive these gifts from God. In Isaiah 6:9–10, God tells Isaiah to give this paradoxical decree as a riddle to the proud people of Israel who had rejected his word: "Keep on hearing, but do not understand; keep on seeing, but do not perceive." After speaking the parable of the sower to the crowds in Matthew 13:1–9, Jesus recalls this damning decree in his explanation of his parables to his disciples in 13:10–17. There he teaches them that the capacity to hear God's word with understanding is given by God to those who are ready to receive it as a gift from him (Matt 13:11–12). Since the disciples of Jesus have ears to hear and eyes to see, they are much more blessed than the prophets and the righteous people in the Old Testament. That teaching helps them understand the challenging directive that Jesus had given to the crowds and would later give to them too: "Let anyone with ears [to hear] listen" (Matt 13:9, 43 NRSV). God gives the gift of hearing through his word. Like the man who was deaf and mute, we all receive the ability to hear God's word with understanding as a gift from him. Jesus gives us hearing ears by opening them up for us.

# YOU HAVE CAUSED
## ALL HOLY SCRIPTURES
## TO BE WRITTEN
## FOR OUR LEARNING

# V

# SPEAKING WITH AUTHORITY

*His word was with authority.*

*Luke 4:32 NKJV*

**D**ifferent authority! Different power! Spiritual authority! Spiritual power! That's why the impact of God's speech differs from the impact of human speech. That's why the Bible differs from all other books.

There are, broadly speaking, two kinds of personal power—power that empowers others and power that disempowers them. On the one hand, there is self-assertive, unbridled, independent power, coercive power that enforces obedience and compliance. By the exercise of such power, people gain and retain power for themselves at the expense of others. It is essentially abusive because it comes from disempowering them. It is all too often used to manipulate and bully, oppress and exploit, harass and destroy them. The power of the evildoers and the devil is like that.

On the other hand, there is authorized, conferred, dependent power—constructive power that is used to benefit others and empower them. Those who exercise that kind of benevolent power can do so because, like policemen and judges, they have been authorized to act in a limited capacity with the responsibility for definite tasks. They have the authority to speak and the power to act as long as they remain under authority and accountable to those who have authority over them. People who are under authority increase their authority by delegating it to others. They gain in power as they use it to empower others. The power of God and Jesus is like that.

Like the words of the prophets and the words of the apostles, the words of Jesus had the power to do what he said because they were the words of his heavenly Father that he translated into human speech. As God's incarnate Son he was a man under authority. He did not speak and act in his own right but in obedience to God. And that is why he spoke with authority and power, the authority of God the Father and the power of the Holy Spirit.

There are two stories that show what kind of authority Jesus had. The first is recorded early in the ministry of Jesus, in Mark 1:21–27. After calling his first four disciples, Jesus takes them into the synagogue in Capernaum and teaches the gospel to the assembled congregation. As they hear what he has to say, the people are astonished because he teaches them with self-evident authority. They are even more astonished when he uses his authority to drive out an unclean spirit from a man with two simple commands: "Be silent, and come out of him" (1:25). The authority of Jesus was verbal and spiritual. He used it to teach God's word and save a spiritually disempowered man.

The second story is recorded in Matthew 8:5–13. It is the story of a Roman centurion who begs Jesus to heal his paralyzed, pain-stricken servant. When Jesus agrees to accompany the centurion in order to heal his servant (8:7), the centurion insists that Jesus should not visit his home because he is unworthy of him and does not need a visit from him. Since he believes in the promise that Jesus has given, he realizes that a simple word from Jesus is all that is needed to heal his servant. He says, "Only say the word, and my servant will be healed" (8:8). The reason for the centurion's reliance on a word spoken by Jesus is that, like his rank in the Roman army and allegiance to the Roman emperor, Jesus can exercise divine authority, because he is a man under divine authority. That is why his word has the power to heal his servant. Jesus therefore commends him for his faith in his promise and heals his servant by saying, "Go; let it be done for you as you have believed" (8:13). By his decree Jesus heals the centurion's servant. Because Jesus has divine authority, his word has the power to create faith and to heal. See also the use of the same decree for two blind men in Matthew 9:29 and of a similar decree for the Canaanite woman with a demon-possessed daughter in 15:28.

The power of Christ's word comes from the authority that God the Father confers on him. The Father delegates his own authority to Jesus; he gives him all authority in heaven and earth (Matt 28:18), the authority over all humanity (John 17:2). He authorizes Jesus to speak and act on his behalf. Thus in John 12:49 Jesus says, "I have not spoken on my own authority, but the Father who sent me has himself given me a commandment—what to say and what to do." Later he adds (14:10), "The words that I say to you I do not speak on my own authority, but the Father who dwells in me does his works [through them]." Because Jesus speaks on behalf of his Father and under his authority, the Father does his work through the words of Jesus. This is so because Jesus does not speak his own word but the word of the Father who sent him (John 14:24).

Jesus was authorized to do his Father's work and speak the Father's word. He had the authority to sacrifice his own life to save the lives of his disciples (John 10:18). He therefore also now has the authority to forgive sins (Matt 9:6, 8) and cast out demons (Mark 1:27), the authority to heal sickness and disease (Matt 10:1) and give eternal life to all believers (John 17:2). Since he has divine authority to pass judgment, he gives eternal life to all who hear his word and believe in him (John 5:19–30). Those who reject his life-giving word and refuse to believe in him condemn themselves to eternal death (John 3:17–18; 5:29; 12:47–48). They are like terminally sick people who refuse to accept the medical treatment that could save their lives. They bring death on themselves.

J ust as the authority of Jesus differs from human authority, so the power of his words differs in its effect from the power of human speech. The impact of human speech depends on the spirit of those who speak it—their personality and vitality, their affability and energy, their confidence and intelligence, their expressiveness and impressiveness, their winsomeness and wit. But the impact of divine speech depends on God's Spirit. Like the breath of a human speaker, the Holy Spirit animates God's word. Inspired as it is by the Holy Spirit, his word inspires both the speaker and the hearer with the same Spirit. The Holy Spirit empowers God's word so that it does what it says and gives what it promises.

God's word is spiritually effective and powerful because it is combined with his Spirit. That's what makes it different from my words. So, for example, if I visit a sick patient in the hospital and say, "Get well!" nothing much happens. At best, my words may cheer the patient for a little while. But when Jesus says the same words to sick people, they are healed. Same words—different effect! The difference is that the words of Jesus are spoken with divine authority and divine power, the power of the Holy Spirit. They work a miracle. In fact, miracles commonly happen wherever he proclaims the gospel with divine authority. They provide evidence of his identity and authority (Luke 7:18–23).

John sums up the connection between God's word and the gift of his Spirit in this way: "He whom God has sent utters the words of God, for he gives the Spirit without measure. The

Father loves the Son and has given all things into his hands"
(3:34–35). The first "he" is meant to be taken in two ways. It
first refers to Jesus and then to each of his apostles and ministers. This describes how God the Father delivers his spiritual
gifts from heaven to earth. We have a verbal chain of transmission from the Father to the Son, and from the Son to his disciples, and from them to other disciples. That chain of giving is
based on the love of the Father for his Son. Since he loves his
Son, he holds nothing back from him but gives all that he has
to him and to those who belong to his Son.

So, on one hand, God has sent his Son to speak his words
and give his Spirit to people on earth, the people God gives
him as his disciples. By speaking these words, the Son gives the
Spirit to them as they listen to him. And that without measure,
completely and entirely! Through the words that he speaks
and the Spirit that he gives as he speaks, the Son delivers the
Father's gifts to them. On the other hand, God the Father, even
more amazingly, also commissions other people to join Jesus
in bringing God's Spirit and all his gifts to others by speaking the words of God to them. Those who hear these words
and believe in them receive the Spirit and everything else that
belongs to Jesus.

Jesus has the authority of his Father and power of the Holy
Spirit to save those who hear his word and believe in him. He
was not authorized to inaugurate a social-political revolution
but to rescue people from sin and death and equip them to work

together with him as members of God's royal family. He does not use his authority to coerce them to serve him but to deliver heavenly gifts to them. As the incarnate word of his divine Father, he confers his own filial status and spiritual resources on them. Through his word he gives them the authority, the right, and power to be children of God (John 1:12). His word has the authority and power to accomplish all that.

The prayer of Jesus for his disciples in John 17 refers to this divine order for the distribution of heavenly gifts on earth. God the Father has given the Son authority to give eternal life to people on earth (17:2); he has given Jesus his work to do (17:4); he has given him his name (17:12), his glory as God's Son (17:22), his words (17:8, 14), and his disciples (17:6, 9, 24). Jesus, in turn, gives his disciples his glory as God's Son by giving them his Father's name (17:6, 12, 26) and his Father's words (17:8, 14). And the disciples receive all this by receiving his words (17:7) and believing in him (17:20). God's word has the power to accomplish all this. It does not establish a chain of command but a supernatural process of giving and receiving, the means for the transmission and reception of God's love (17:26).

# VI

# THE WORD OF CHRIST

The word is near you, in your
mouth and in your heart.

*Romans 10:8 ESV*

I remember a dramatic incident in a pastors' conference that I attended as a theological student. In a debate on how to apply God's word in preaching, a prominent theologian tried to refocus a rather disjointed, meandering discussion by asserting, "I always preach about Christ and the gospel." In response to that assertion, a colleague of his, a theologian named Hermann Sasse, took the microphone and declared, "In all my life as a pastor I have never ever preached about Christ and the gospel. I have always only ever preached him and his gospel."

By this claim he did not just refer to the need to interpret the whole Bible as testimony to Jesus; he made a much more audacious point. He claimed that the proclamation of God's word was meant to convey Christ and his gifts to its hearers. The gospel of Jesus is not just a message about him; it is a message that offers him to its hearers. That is what it is meant to do. It is the message that brings him to us. Through it the risen Lord Jesus comes to us and gives himself to us. Those who listen to him and to the preachers whom he sends receive him and the Father who sent him (Matt 10:40; Luke 10:16; John 13:20).

Jesus told his disciples on the night before he died that he would not leave them as orphans but would come to them, so that they could see him and share in life with him; Jesus would share the Father's love with them by manifesting himself to them (John 14:19–20). When Jude asked him how he could manifest himself to them rather than the world, Jesus made this stunning announcement: "If anyone loves me, he will keep my word and my Father will love him, and we will come to him and make our home with him. Whoever does not love me does not keep my word. And the word that you hear is not mine but the Father's who sent me" (14:23–24). After his death and resurrection, the word of Jesus would be the way by which he would not just come to visit them but would also come to cohabit with them. Through his word, both he and his Father would come to make their home with them here on earth in anticipation of their home with him in heaven (John 14:2–7). The Father therefore shows and tells his love to us through the word of Jesus. If we love Jesus and listen to his word, the Father will love us as he loves his Son. Through faith in his word we will receive Jesus and his heavenly Father as they come to be with us. For Jesus, as for every lover, words are the means for self-giving and self-disclosure. The word of Jesus is the word of his Father. It discloses them both to us. It brings both of them to us.

It is true that God's word tells us about Jesus; it does give us information about Jesus. But it is meant to do much more for us than that. By its proper proclamation, Jesus preaches himself to those who hear it (Eph 2:17), just as he preached himself to the skeptical congregation in Capernaum at the beginning of his ministry (Luke 4:16–21), and explained what was said about him in all the Scriptures to the two disheartened disciples on the road to Emmaus on the evening of Easter (Luke 24:27). The word that he speaks to us cannot be separated from his proximity, his real presence with us. He is both the messenger and the message. His word has its effect from his presence with us. By his word he does not just tell us what he has done, but he proclaims what he is now doing for us and giving to us. It is good news for us, because he is here with us to make contact and keep contact with us through its proclamation.

I n the ancient world, kings communicated with their people by the messengers they sent. These messengers stood in for them and represented them. They were the king's heralds, heralds of good news from him and about him, good news of events such as his coronation and the birth of an heir to the throne, his amnesty for political prisoners and debtors in taxation, his victory over his enemies and his impending visit with them. The last kind of proclamation was most welcome for ordinary people, because the king's herald would not only tell them of his impending visit but also announce his actual arrival and his presence with them to receive their petitions and bestow favors on them.

The New Testament uses the Greek term for the visit of a king to announce the message of our salvation. It describes the proclamation of the imminent coming of the Messiah by John the Baptist (Mark 1:4) as well as the announcement by Jesus of the arrival of God's kingly rule with him as the Messiah (Mark 1:14–15). It also describes the proclamation of the risen Lord Jesus by the evangelists and apostles in the early church (e.g., Acts 8:18; 9:20). They announced his presence to deliver heavenly gifts to people on earth. Thus in 2 Corinthians 1:19, Paul asserts that he and his fellow pastors Silvanus and Timothy proclaimed Jesus present among the people in Corinth as their King and God's royal Son. A little later, in 4:5–6, he adds this about their proclamation of the gospel: "What we proclaim is not ourselves, but Jesus Christ as Lord, with ourselves as your servants. For God, who said, 'Let light shine out of darkness,' has shone in your hearts to give the light of the knowledge of the glory of God in the face of Jesus Christ." God's glory is his manifest, accessible presence with his people in Jesus. Their preaching, therefore, disclosed the hidden radiance, the enlightening presence of both Jesus and God the Father to the Christians in Corinth. It brought their hearers face-to-face with Jesus, so they were able to see God's glory reflected in him.

In Romans 10:5–17, Paul explains how Christ reaches out to people through the proclamation of the gospel. He bases his teaching on God's command to his people in Deuteronomy 30:11–14, his life-giving mandate for them, his gift of life to them through his word, and their attention to his voice in it (Deut 30:10, 12, 16). Paul focuses on the mention by Moses of the nearness of God's word with them, its availability to them and intimacy with them in their mouths and in their hearts, for them to hear it and do it. So too for the new people of God! The word of Christ and Christ himself are now present in the mouths and hearts of believers. They do not need to ascend into heaven to bring Christ down to earth for them, because he has come to earth for all people in his incarnation; they do not need to descend into his grave to bring him to life again for them, because God the Father has raised him from the dead. Rather, the risen Lord Jesus Christ is now as close to them here on earth as his word, the word that brings him to them as they listen to him and believe in him, the word that they have in their hearts and in their mouths.

Through the proclamation of his resurrection and their faith in him, they receive him and his blessings. As they hear the word of Christ proclaimed to them, it enters their hearts and makes them believers; it gives them life through their faith in him and reliance on him. Since the word of Christ has become the word of faith for them—the word that produces and nourishes their faith—they can confess him as their Lord by calling on him for their salvation and all the riches that he provides.

The word of Christ that proclaims him to them in their hearts combines with the word of faith that they confess. Taken together, they form the bridge by which he comes to them, so that they can come to him.

Paul explains how people can come to Christ to receive him and his gifts (Rom 10:14–17). There are four parts to the bridge of faith that God provides for them through the gospel. People cannot call on Jesus unless they believe in him; people cannot believe in him unless they hear the gospel; people cannot hear the gospel unless someone preaches it to them; people cannot preach the gospel unless they are sent by God. Here everything is given as a gift from God. Here everything depends on faith in Christ and his word. Here everything depends on hearing and receiving Christ in and with his word.

Through the gospel, Christ comes to deliver himself and his gifts to those who put their trust in him. Origen, the influential biblical scholar and teacher in the early church, says this in his *Commentary on the Gospel of John*: "What the Gospels say is to be regarded in the light of promises of good things. And we must say that the good things the apostles announce in this Gospel are simply Jesus."[1] That fact determines how we are meant to hear what he says in the four Gospels and how we should read the whole Bible. We approach his word with open-hearted faith that is ready to receive him and what he offers us. Without the gospel of Jesus and faith in him, we misappropriate the word of God. Martin Luther describes this most eloquently and memorably in "A Brief Instruction on What to Look For and Expect in the Gospels." This is what he says there:

> When you open the book containing the gospels and read or hear how Christ comes here or there, or how someone is brought to him, you should therein perceive the sermon or the gospel through which he is coming to you, or you are being brought to him. For the preaching of the gospel is nothing else than Christ coming to us, or we being brought to him. When you see how he works, however, and how he helps everyone to whom he comes or who is brought to him, then rest assured that faith is accomplishing this in you and that he is offering your soul exactly the same sort of help and favor through the gospel. If you pause here and let him do you good, that is, if you believe that he benefits and helps you, then you really have it. Then Christ is yours, presented to you as a gift.[2]

# GRANT THAT WE
# MAY SO HEAR THEM

# VII

# GOD'S WORD SAVES

*To you the word of this salvation has been sent.*
*Acts 13:26 NKJV*

**A**m I saved? If so, how, and from what? If not, what must I do to be saved? These are not idle, theoretical questions. The answer to them is a very practical matter, a matter of spiritual life or death. It can provide me with a sure basis for my life on earth or doom me to lifelong uncertainty.

The issue becomes acute for conscientious people when it is taught that salvation is based on a single experience of conversion at a particular time and place in their lives. If that is so, then they can only be sure that they are saved if they have had that experience. Their assurance of salvation depends on it.

Let me illustrate this from what happened to my wife Claire as a young woman. She experienced a conversion on three distinct occasions. When she was thirteen, she stood up in her religion class to confess her need for Jesus to cleanse her from sin, after a visiting preacher had used the book of Leviticus to speak of a holy God who demanded a sacrifice for sin and of Jesus who offered himself to atone for all sin. At the age of fifteen, she attended a Billy Graham crusade in which she was once again cut to the heart and moved to make a decision for Jesus. At the age of nineteen, she joined a youth rally where she once again committed herself to Jesus because she realized that she had failed to trust in God to direct the future course of her life. These three events left her in a state of uncertainty, because she could not say which was her true conversion. She, therefore, was not sure that she was saved. It left her spiritually unsettled because she doubted whether any of them was a real conversion. The issue remained unresolved until she discovered Luther's teaching that Christians were justified sinners. As such they were involved in a daily and lifelong experience of conversion that would only be completed at their physical death and resurrection. So she realized that she was not just converted on one occasion but on all three and many other occasions. What's more, she discovered that both her salvation and her assurance of salvation did not depend on her personal commitment to him or her subjective experience of it, but on Christ and his saving word, the word that had saved her, was saving her, and would save her, the word that saved her from all evil powers and kept her safe from them.

In the introduction of his Letter to the Romans, Paul has this to say about that word: "I am not ashamed of the gospel, for it is the power of God for salvation to everyone who believes, to the Jew first and also to the Greek" (1:16–17). The accent here is on the exercise of divine power through the proclamation of the gospel. Paul tells us three things about the gospel: the reason for its power, the purpose of its power, and the recipients of salvation by its power.

First, the gospel is the power of God. By it and with it God exercises his divine power in a unique way, the power of his Holy Spirit (Rom 1:4), the power of him "who gives life to the dead and calls into existence the things that do not exist" (Rom 4:17). Its effect does not depend on the ability of the person who preaches it, or on the ability of its hearers to appropriate it. Its impact depends on God alone. Those who experience its power do so from a position of spiritual weakness and powerlessness. They have nothing to offer to God except their empty hands; they have everything to receive from him. Through the divine power of the gospel God acts on them and works in them.

Second, the gospel has the power to accomplish salvation. God exercises his power in other ways besides the gospel. Through his decrees he not only creates the universe with all that is in it but also upholds it and governs it. Through his law with its commandments and prohibitions, he shows what he requires of all people, discloses their guilt, and leads them to repentance. But, despite all its moral and spiritual power, the law is unable to save sinners and put them right with God, because it relies on them and their meager resources for its fulfillment. Like a cripple that I command to walk, or a corpse that I tell to live, sinful people cannot carry out its demands. Due to their spiritual inability and disability, the law cannot free them from the chains of sin. Only the gospel, the good news of salvation, has the power to do that and give that to them. It alone has the power to save sinners from eternal doom and give life to people who are otherwise dead in trespasses and sins. The gospel is the power of God for salvation, the word that pardons sin and justifies repentant sinners. It does not just tell about the salvation that Jesus won by his sacrificial death for them and resurrection for their justification, but it actually delivers the free gift of salvation to them wherever they may be. It saves those who cannot save themselves. It is the word by which they are now being saved (1 Cor 15:2); it is the word by which they will be saved (Acts 11:14).

Third, the gospel offers and conveys the salvation that Jesus gained for all people to every believer. While the gospel makes salvation available to all people who are all equally powerless, it is received by those who believe in it. Salvation and faith belong together intrinsically, like the giving of a gift and its reception. Whereas the proclamation of the gospel is the divine means, God's hand by which he offers salvation, the faith that hears it and believes in it is the empty human hand that receives it and experiences its saving power. So, from a human point of view, salvation comes from faith in the gospel, which is given for the creation and promotion of faith in it (Rom 1:17).

The proclamation of the gospel begins with Jesus and is continued by him. Its proclamation had been foretold by the prophet Isaiah. He said that the gospel would announce the salvation of God, his victory and peace, his presence with his people, and his reign as King over all the earth (Isa 52:7–10). The coming Messiah, the heir of David, would be anointed with God's Spirit to preach the gospel to the poor people who depended on God for salvation from brokenhearted dejection and crushing oppression, from incarceration and injustice, from guilt and grief and shame (Isa 61:1–4). God would commission him to preach the gospel that would save them. So in keeping with these prophecies, Jesus, after his baptism, preached the gospel of God, first by himself (Mark 1:14; Acts 10:36–38) and then through the apostles and other preachers (Luke 24:46–47; Heb 2:3).

We have this succinct summary of the gospel from Jesus himself in Mark 1:15 (NRSV): "The time is fulfilled, and the kingdom of God has come near; repent, and believe in the good news." Jesus tells us three things in this proclamation. First, Jesus announces that the pivotal event in world history and the history of Israel has happened with the arrival of God's kingdom— God's defeat of all the evil powers that opposed his kingship, his triumphant rule over them, and his long-awaited reign of mercy and grace, justice and righteousness, pardon and peace on earth. With that a new age had begun, the age of salvation.

Second, Jesus announces that he himself ushers in God's kingdom. He therefore declares that he is the Messiah, God's royal Son. Where and when he preaches the gospel, the kingdom comes. He brings in God's kingdom by his proclamation of the gospel, the gospel of the kingdom (Matt 4:23; 9:35; 24:14; Luke 4:23; 8:1). By his proclamation of that gospel, Jesus actually ushers in God's rule, so that those who hear it can enjoy life with God as sons and daughters of the heavenly King.

Third, Jesus includes a call to repent and believe in the gospel as the way by which people receive the kingdom as a gift from God (Luke 12:32; 22:29). Repentance and faith belong together; repentance involves returning to God and trusting in him, just as sin has to do with turning away from him by mistrust in him and his word. By trusting in the gospel, they turn away from themselves and their sins, and turn back to God and his word to receive what he gives them through the gospel. They can return to God because he has sent his Son to bring them back to himself, like the lost sheep, the lost coin, and the lost sons in Luke 15. They discover that he has come to seek and save the lost (Luke 19:10).

Mark tells how that happens, simply and practically, with the story of the call of the first four disciples after this proclamation of the gospel of God (1:16–20). Jesus calls them by saying, "Follow me, and I will make you fishers of people" (1:17). With those words he calls them to repent by putting their trust in him personally as he leads them on the way of salvation. That powerful call has an immediate effect on them. They leave their nets and their colleagues and follow Jesus. Unlike the Pharisees who taught that God's kingdom would come by way of obedience to the laws and its demands, they enter the kingdom by way of faith in Jesus and the gospel. They receive it as a gift from him (Mark 10:15).

In his ministry, from his baptism to his death on the cross, Jesus brought salvation in word and deed to people who needed help from God. Thus the four Gospels tell how Jesus, after God the Father had anointed him with the Holy Spirit and power, "went about doing good and healing all who were oppressed by the devil" (Acts 11:37). He saved different people in different circumstances from the different kinds of evil that threatened to blight their lives and destroy them, such as hunger and drowning, disabilities and infirmities, oppression by the devil and evil spirits, social rejection and fear of God's condemnation, sin, and even death itself. All these temporal acts of salvation anticipated and foreshadowed their eternal salvation from condemnation to eternal death and destruction in the last judgment. And all that through Jesus and his word, the message of salvation.

The risen Lord Jesus continues to preach the gospel of salvation through his apostles and their successors (Eph 2:17). The apostles did not merely bear witness to what Jesus said and did before his sacrificial death for the salvation of the world; they also testify to what he continues to say and do after his resurrection and ascension (Acts 1:1; Heb 2:3). We can ascertain how this happens from the sermon that Paul gave on a Sabbath in the synagogue at Antioch in Pisidia (Acts 13:16–41). There he, as the slave girl in Philippi with a spirit of divination later declared (Acts 16:17), proclaimed "the word of salvation" to an audience of Jews and God-fearing gentiles. His message of salvation unfolds in three parts: a summary of how God saved his people, from their rescue from slavery in Egypt to his choice of David as their king, with a focus in 13:23 on Jesus as Israel's promised Savior (13:16–25); the fulfillment of all God's promises of salvation by the death and resurrection of Jesus (13:26–35); and the proclamation of the forgiveness of sins for believers with a warning against the dire consequence of its rejection (13:38–41).

There are two sides, two dimensions to the proclamation of this message, one human and visible, the other divine and invisible. On the one hand, Paul preaches the good news of salvation to the congregation in the synagogue (13:32). He proclaims the message that God kept his promise to bring a Savior to Israel by sending Jesus, and that he fulfilled the promise of salvation in a way that was hard to believe by raising Jesus from death and physical corruption (13:26–37). On the other hand, Paul's sermon culminates in this amazing announcement: "Let it be known to you therefore, brothers, that through this man forgiveness of sins is proclaimed to you, and by him everyone who believes is justified and freed from everything from which you could not be justified and freed from the law of Moses." As is often the case in the New Testament, the use of these passive verbs tells what God does in a hidden way through human agents. So through the message of salvation that Paul preaches, God proclaims the gospel to the people in the synagogue. God proclaims the gospel *through* the man Jesus. That gospel is pronouncement of divine pardon *by* Jesus, God's forgiveness of sins, his release for people from sins, his justification of those who believe in Jesus, and his liberation of them from their transgressions of God's law. Just as Jesus had freed a paralyzed man and a sinful woman by saying, "Your sins are forgiven" (Mark 2:5; Luke 7:48), so Jesus comes to free the people in that synagogue from the guilt and power of sin by his proclamation of forgiveness. That word of pardon anticipates the sentence of the divine Judge in his final judgment. Those who hear it and believe it are therefore free from all condemnation. It sets those who trust in it free from their three worst enemies—the guilt of sin that alienates them from God and each other, the penalty of death for the transgression of God's law, and the devil who uses God's law to condemn them.

Who then preaches the gospel? Paul does! Jesus does! God the Father does! Through Paul as his spokesman, Jesus preaches the gospel, the message of salvation, the good news of forgiveness to the congregation in the synagogue. By preaching the gospel, he delivers God's pardon to those who believe in Jesus and his word of salvation.

The message of salvation is hard to believe (Acts 13:41) because God accomplishes it through the crucifixion of Jesus. It declares that God saves people from death by the condemnation of his Son and his shameful death on the cross. Paul explores this paradox at some length in 1 Corinthians 1:17–31. God saves people through the crucifixion of Christ Jesus and the proclamation of salvation with "the word of the cross" (1:18). Those who believe in him are saved by him. Paul therefore maintains that "the word of the cross is folly to those who are perishing, but to us who are being saved it is the power of God" (1:18). In his wisdom, God chooses to exercise his power to save through weakness, the weakness of his Son and the weakness of his word, the weakness of lowly people and the weakness of their faith. Paul concludes, "God chose what is foolish in the world to shame the wise; God chose what is weak in the world to shame the strong; God chose what is low and despised in the world, even things that are not, to bring to nothing things that are, so that no human being might boast in the presence of God" (1:27–29). Yet those who believe in Christ crucified can boast in him, because they have their salvation in him; in him they have "righteousness and sanctification and redemption" (1:30). They have nothing in themselves and receive everything from him. They depend on borrowed power for their salvation, the power that is made perfect in their weakness (2 Cor 12:9).

Although our salvation was won for us by Jesus once and for all time with his death and resurrection, it was not delivered to us there and then. It is conveyed to us here and now through the gospel and received by us through faith in it. That does not occur, as my wife was taught, at only one point in our lives. To be sure, it is not delivered to us piecemeal but entirely in Jesus. Yet we keep on receiving it from him for as long as we live and receive it entirely only at our death and resurrection.

We are called to a life of repentance and renewal as we die daily to sin and are raised to life with Jesus. We therefore always depend on Christ and his word for our salvation. He leads us as we follow him on the way of salvation, the way of faith in him and lifelong listening to him.

That truth is taught most simply by James in 1:21. After warning his congregation against the danger of self-righteous anger, he says, "Therefore put away all filthiness and rampant growth of wickedness and receive with meekness the implanted word that is able to save your souls." He uses a picture from horticulture to illustrate our ongoing dependence on God's word for our salvation. There are two phases in the life of a fruit tree. The seed of the tree is planted in the soil, and then the tree grows as it receives its life from the seed. So too in the life of the disciple! God plants his word in our hearts when we hear it. He gives it to us as a gift. Yet that is not the end of the matter for us. What we hear is of little or no use unless we receive it as God's word and what it offers as his gift to us. So the New Testament emphasizes the reception of God's word in a number of places (Acts 8:14; 11:1; 17:11; 1 Thess 1:6; 2:13). In humility we need to receive it and what it offers to us, so that we can grow and become fruitful. That is a process of ongoing reception, because we lack the power to gain our salvation, let alone produce the fruit of our salvation. Only God's word has the power to save our souls. It is the word that saves us and keeps us safe.

# VIII

# GOD'S WORD GIVES LIFE

Lord, to whom shall we go? You
have the words of eternal life.

*John 6:68 ESV*

The living dead are all around us. I do not refer to zombies or ghosts, even though the living dead may be something like them. They are not the people who are unconscious or in a coma, or those who have lost their minds, or even the host of those who are emotionally dead. Rather, they are people who are spiritually dead, people who are dead in trespasses and sins (Eph 2:1). They are not strangers to us because we too were once one of them, and we still are haunted by the imprint of that condition on us—so much so that we often feel less than fully alive. We do not notice them because they do not seem to be dead. From a human point of view, they are physically alive and filled with much apparent vitality. Yet they are dead, as dead to God as a corpse is to those whose life it had once shared.

They are spiritually dead because they have rejected God (Rom 6:23). Like Adam and Eve, they have refused to listen to God's word of warning and have eaten the deadly fruit of the forbidden tree (Gen 2:17; 3:1–11). By their rebellion they have cut themselves off, like a branch from a tree, from the spiritual life that God provides for them. They have committed a kind of spiritual suicide because they did not want to depend on God for their spiritual vitality; they wanted to be superwomen and supermen who possessed a superlife and its superpowers for themselves.

We too once belonged to the living dead. But the life that began with an earthly birth has been changed by a heavenly rebirth. We who were born to die by our human birth have been born again by water and the Spirit to live with God (John 3:1–9). We have been born again through the living word of God that was announced as good news to us in baptism (1 Pet 1:3, 23–25). That word is an imperishable seed of life for us, something that remains sown in us and produces new life in us. God the Father, the giver of every good and perfect gift, "chose to give us birth through the word of truth, that we might be a kind of firstfruits of all he created" (Jas 1:18). He did that for us in baptism. There we who were born as children of Adam became children of God, brothers and sisters of Jesus and sons and daughters of his heavenly Father. So, like the risen Lord Jesus, we now belong to God's new creation (2 Cor 5:17). Together with Jesus the firstborn from the dead (Col 1:18), we are the firstfruits of

God's new creation. Our rebirth anticipates the renewal of the old creation. We see an allusion to this in the New Testament with the use of the regeneration by Jesus for God's creation of a new world in Matthew 19:28 and by Paul for God's creation of a new person through baptism in Titus 3:4–7.

Just as Adam was created by God's word, we have been re-created by it. Just as God breathed the breath of life into Adam (Gen 2:7), so Jesus breathes the Holy Spirit into us by saying, "Receive the Holy Spirit" (John 20:22). We have been raised from death to life together with Jesus. By sharing in Christ's death and resurrection through baptism, we have been made alive together with Jesus (Rom 6:4; Eph 2:5). We have been brought from death apart from God to life together with him (Rom 6:13). And that already now in this life through the life-giving word of Jesus, the one whose words are Spirit and life (John 6:63).

Like many naïve Christians, I, when I was young, fancied that Christ offered me two main things: forgiveness now in this life as a ticket to heaven and life after death when I died. Little did I realize then that both these gifts also impinged on my present existence. Then in my late teens I was shaken by the sudden, premature death of the mother of a close friend. This confronted me with my mortality for the first time. In a state of spiritual turmoil, I read the whole Gospel of John and noted all the references to life in it. As I read it, one passage caught my attention and spoke to me personally. So much so that it has, ever since, become a kind of catchword and motto for me, my spiritual lodestar. It is this solemn declaration by Jesus: "Truly, truly, whoever hears my word and believes him who sent me has eternal life. He does not come into judgment, but has already passed from death to life" (John 5:24). I found it hard to take in and understand what I read. In fact, I am still taking it in and receiving what Jesus offers to me and requires of me with these words. He says that I shall never see death, let alone taste its temporal and eternal bitterness (John 8:51–52). If that promise is true, and I have no reason to believe that it is false, then Jesus is offering me eternal life already now. And even better than that, he promises that if I listen to his word and believe in it as the word that his Father sent him to proclaim, I need never fear any word of judgment and condemnation from him—neither now, nor ever again!

My amazing discovery was this: As disciples of Jesus who believe in him and what he says, our reception and enjoyment of eternal life depends on him and his word. Through faith in his word, we have eternal life already now, life before death as well as life after death. Like the Israelites whom God delivered from the land of slavery and death and brought into life with him in the promised land, we have passed from death into life. Death is now behind us! There is nothing but life before us. So we do not journey from rapidly diminishing life into death, but we travel with Jesus through death into life, increasing and unending life, more and more life, superabundant life. And all that through the life-giving word of Jesus!

Our life story is much the same as the stories of the people who were about to die or had died in the four Gospels. Think of the official's son in John 4:46–54 who was at the point of death, and how he was restored to life by the promise of Jesus to his father: "Go; your son will live." Think of the only daughter of Jairus in Luke 8:40–42, 48–56, who died before Jesus could reach her, and how he said, "Child, arise." Think of the only son of the widow in Nain in Luke 7:10–17, who had died and was taken out to be buried, and how Jesus revived him with the command, "Young man, I say to you, arise" (7:16). Think of the death of Lazarus, the friend of Jesus, in John 11:1–46, who was dead and had been buried for four days, and how Jesus brought him back to life by saying, "Lazarus, come out" (11:43). Like each of these, we have been revived and are kept alive by Christ's word.

God's word is the living word of the living God (Heb 4:13; 1 Pet 1:13). That applies to all that he has to say through Moses and the prophets in the Old Testament and Jesus and his apostles in the New Testament. God speaks life-giving utterances, words that give physical life to all living creatures and spiritual life to God's people. Thus in Deuteronomy 8:3 Moses asserts that people live by every word that comes from the mouth of God. His word gives them life and keeps them alive. All the words that God speaks to Moses, whether they are his ordinances for human life on earth (Lev 18:3) or the promises that he attaches to the commandments to his people for life with him in the promised land (Deut 6:2, 24; 8:2; 30:15–20; 32:47–48), are living utterances (Acts 7:28). His word is their life (Deut 32:47) because he himself is their life (Deut 30:20). That is why the author of Psalm 119 looks for life from God's word (119:25, 50, 93, 107, 116, 144, 156, 159). All his meditations on God's word culminate in the plea "Let my soul live" (119:175). Nevertheless the words of Moses and the prophets do not in and of themselves deliver eternal life, heavenly life for people in the new world, new life in the age to come. That can only be had from Jesus (John 5:37–40). He gives what is promised to God's people in the old covenant (Acts 13:32–33). He speaks the words of eternal life first to his apostles (John 6:68) and then through them to others (Acts 5:20; Phil 2:16; 1 John 1:1–2). The gift of eternal life that God had promised to give to his people through Daniel (12:2) is now revealed through Christ's word (Titus 1:2–3).

We therefore depend on Jesus for the spiritual life that we now enjoy. The Holy Spirit—and the life the Holy Spirit brings— is available to us only in Christ. And he gives this life to us through his word and by faith in his word. Thus our spiritual vitality does not come from our spiritual self-development but depends on our faith in him. Because we are joined to Christ, we continually receive our life from him. We share in his life as God's Son by faith in his word.

Jesus himself teaches how we receive eternal life from him most vividly in John's Gospel. He was commissioned by his heavenly Father to give eternal life to his disciples (12:50; 17:2).

He came to reside on earth to give life to its inhabitants, abundant life, life in all its fullness, his own divine life as the Son of the Father (John 10:10). He laid down his own life by his death and took it up again by his resurrection, to bring them into life with his heavenly Father (10:11–18). He gives that life to all those whom he calls to be his disciples (5:21; 10:28), to those whom the Father gives to him (17:3). Through faith in Jesus they have eternal life on earth already now (3:15–16, 36; 6:40, 47). Eternal life begins as soon as they hear his word and believe in him (5:24). Through his word, he gives them his life-giving Spirit (3:34–35; 6:63). He produces spiritual life in them by giving them a new birth (3:5–8); he sustains this life by nourishing them with his own flesh and blood (6:53–58).

Yet Jesus does not just give eternal life; eternal life is in him (1:4). He does not just feed people with heavenly food; he himself is the bread of life (6:32–35, 48), the living, life-giving bread that has come down from heaven (6:50–51). He does not just teach the way to life with God; he is the way to life with God because he is that life (14:6). Most remarkably, he presents himself to Martha and all his disciples with this declaration and promise: "I am the resurrection and the life. Whoever believes in me, though he die, yet shall he live, and whoever lives and believes in me shall never die" (11:25–26). So Jesus gives us life through his word because he offers himself with his life to us in it. We receive life from him because we believe in him and depend on him.

J esus does not offer us superhuman life; he does not turn us into supermen and superwomen with extraordinary physical and mental powers. Instead, he swaps places with us. He joins us in our human life on earth so that we can join him in his life with God the Father (John 17:24). By our union with Jesus, we share in his sonship, just as a woman who marries a man joins his family and receives his father as her father. His position with God the Father and his access to the Father, his status and all his privileges as God's only Son, the Father's love for him and his love for the Father—all these are ours through our faith in Jesus (17:20–28). Yet we do not possess these gifts by ourselves and in ourselves; we have them only as we receive them from Jesus. We have eternal life by believing in him and receiving it from Him. In short, we borrow it from him, for he alone has the words of eternal life (6:68).

In the conclusion of his Gospel, John takes this one step further. He tells his hearers and readers that his whole Gospel was written so that they would have faith in Jesus as the Messiah, the Son of God, and that they would have life by believing in him. Its purpose, its function, was to convey the gift of life to them through what he writes (20:30–31). We could add and should add that this is the function of all the books that make up the Scriptures. Each in its own way tells us how our Savior, Christ Jesus, "has abolished death and brought life and immortality to light through the gospel" (2 Tim 1:10). That is the gospel they proclaim. That is what we are meant to receive from the whole Bible.

# READ, MARK, LEARN, AND INWARDLY DIGEST THEM

# IX

# GOD'S WORD NOURISHES

*Your words were found, and I ate
them, and your words became for me
a joy and the delight of my heart.*

*Jeremiah 15:16 ESV*

**T**he books of the Bible originated in an oral culture, a world where people usually communicated by speaking and hearing. That is why Jesus taught verbally and orally. So too the priests and the prophets and the sages in the Old Testament as well as the apostles, evangelists, and teachers in the New Testament. To be sure, there were some people who could read and fewer people who were scribes, people who could read and write well. Yet, even for them, that was not their normal way of interacting with others. So, for example, most literate people, like Paul, did not write their own letters (Gal 6:10; Col 4:16; 2 Thess 3:17), but dictated them to a scribe, and the people who received them either read them aloud or, more commonly, had them read aloud by a scribe for them to hear it, just as we still read books to our children before they can read and even after they can read.

Four things follow from this that are relevant for our understanding and use of the Bible. First, people in the ancient world learned to listen far more attentively than we now do. They needed to memorize what they heard. They learned it by heart so that they could recall it correctly for themselves and report it accurately to others. They depended on their recollection of spoken speech for orientation and security in their social context. Wise people were good speakers because they were first and foremost good listeners. The Bible therefore is not addressed to people who read it but to people who hear what it has to say.

Second, for the people who heard what the Bible had to say, words were basically spoken speech, living words that were spoken face-to-face by a person rather than dead words, letters of the alphabet that had been written down on a manuscript. They were words that were animated by the breath of a living, speaking person and received by the ears of a living, hearing person. They were heard and received in the context of live communication. So we too are meant to take the Bible as spoken speech that is addressed to us.

Third, people in the ancient world did not read a written text, such as a book in the Bible, mentally and silently as we tend to do. Even if they were literate, they read it aloud to themselves, or, more commonly, they had it read aloud to them, so that they could hear what was said and receive what it had to give to them or required of them. As far as we know, the ability to read silently without enunciation came much later. In fact, the earliest record of a person who had developed the skill of silent reading was the famous church father and bishop Ambrose in the third century. People were so amazed by this that they paid to see him reading! We too best hear God's word to us in the Bible by reading it out aloud to ourselves or hearing it read to us.

Fourth, unlike us, people in the ancient world did not separate thinking from speaking and the content of words from the words that had been spoken. For them thinking was a matter of speaking silently to themselves. So, while we speak about what we think or feel, they referred to what they were saying to themselves mentally. Take, for example, the comment of the speaker in Psalm 30:6: "When I felt secure, I said, 'I will never be shaken.' " What's more, the authors of the Bible usually refer to the words that they speak rather than the ideas or theological concepts that they wish to communicate. So, for example, Paul speaks about "the word of reconciliation" rather than the theology of reconciliation (2 Cor 5:19).

We therefore are called to be hearers of God's word rather than critics who analyze and assess it impersonally. There is indeed a place for that. But like the analysis of a love letter, it is of limited value apart from what it offers us and does for us. Like good food, God's words are meant to be received with our ears and digested in our hearts.

T here is a kind of hearing that is much like eating because it has to do with the mouth as well as the ears. The hearer of God's word is meant to assimilate what has been said by speaking it aloud to the ears and through the ears into the heart. In this kind of meditative hearing, people mull over some significant words by repeating them, like a cow with its cud, and letting it address them personally so as to receive what they have to say and give to them.

The notion of hearing with the heart by way of the mouth is described most graphically in Ezekiel 2:8–3:10. In response to the people in exile who refuse to listen to God's word, God commissions Ezekiel to be a prophet in a strange way. He tells Ezekiel to open his mouth to eat what God gives him. Then God gives him a scroll that has his words written on it and tells him to eat that scroll. When Ezekiel eats the scroll with its words of lamentation and mourning and woe, he, like Jeremiah before him (15:16), discovers that it is as sweet as honey to his mouth. After that, God gives this explanation: "Son of man, all the words that I speak to you receive in your heart, and hear with your ears" (3:10). This reverses the usual order of hearing that is followed by taking to heart what has been heard. Ezekiel takes God's words to heart by way of the mouth, so that he can hear them with his ears.

In Psalm 81, God provides verbal nourishment for his people who have assembled as his guests in his presence at the temple to celebrate the Feast of Tabernacles, the great harvest festival at the end of the agricultural year. This prophetic psalm falls into two parts, the call to join in the song that introduces God's speech to his people in 81:1–5 and then the report of his speech to them with its passionate appeal for them to listen to him in 81:6–16. After recalling how he freed their ancestors from hard labor in Egypt (Exod 1:11–14), how he answered their cry for help at the Red Sea (Exod 14:11), and how he provided water for them from the rock at Meribah (Num 20:2–13), God calls on the people who have been feasting on holy meat and bread and wine for the seven days of the harvest festival to hear what he is telling them as he presents himself personally by name to them as their God. He says, "I am the LORD, your God, who brought you out of the land of Egypt. Open your mouth wide, and I will fill it" (Ps 81:10). He offers to fill their mouths with the words of this song and feed them with it. He also promises them that if they will listen to him and follow him, he will feed them with wheat that is more nourishing than manna and satisfy them with honey rather than water from the rock (81:16). They will have the best food to eat and the sweetest beverage to enjoy by listening to his voice.

God gives his word to his people to nourish them. In Deuteronomy 8:1–10, he recalls how he fed them with manna in the desert and promised to bring them into a good land where they would eat bread without scarcity. In that context he also reminds them how he tested them by allowing them to go hungry and thirsty in the desert and by feeding them with manna, in order to teach them that they did not live on bread alone but on every word that came from his mouth (8:3). Just as their physical nourishment depends on physical food, so their spiritual nourishment depends on his word. They therefore must listen to him and attend to his word for their sustenance. Without it they will go hungry (8:3, 16) and thirsty (8:15) and die for lack of sustenance (8:19–20).

In the New Testament, Luke also teaches about the reception of nourishment from God's word with his report of this puzzling exchange between Jesus and a woman in the crowd of bystanders: "As he [Jesus] said this, a woman in the crowd raised her voice and said to him, 'Blessed is the womb that bore you, and the breasts at which you nursed!' But he said, 'Blessed rather are those who hear the word of God and keep it' " (11:27–28).

The woman in the story seems to be a rather earthy and yet pious mother. There's nothing prudish about her and her attitude to motherhood. She seems to be disappointed as a mother by the way her own son—or sons—has turned out. So, when she hears the teaching of Jesus, she envies his mother Mary. She congratulates her for her successful son, who must, of course, take after her and reflect well on her. Like mother like son! How great it would be to have a son like him. Mary is truly blessed to be the mother of Jesus.

In his response to her remark, Jesus does not disagree with her. He admits that Mary is blessed, but he adds that every disciple is even much more blessed than Mary. In fact, Mary is doubly blessed, first as the mother of Jesus and then as a disciple of Jesus. She is most blessed because she hears the word of

God and keeps it. She became pregnant with Jesus by hearing God's word to her and believing in it (Luke 1:38). Yet she is not alone in this. All disciples, including the woman who congratulated Jesus, are just as blessed as Mary, since they, like her, also receive Jesus as their Lord and Savior by trusting in his word.

Jesus compares and contrasts those who receive physical life and nourishment from an earthly mother with those who receive spiritual life and nourishment from God's word. Just as babies receive physical life through their mothers' wombs, so we receive new birth through hearing God's word. His word is our spiritual womb. Yet, like infants, we cannot remain alive without it but also depend on it for our nourishment. Just as babies are nourished with milk from their mothers' breasts, so we are nourished by the same word that regenerated us. The word of God, spoken by Jesus, is our spiritual breast. By holding on to God's word and keeping it in our hearts, we receive ongoing, life-sustaining nourishment from it.

Like infants, we grow up as children of God by feeding on the pure milk of God's word (1 Pet 2:2–3). Yet, if we are to grow up and become spiritually mature, we also need to supplement that basic food with the solid food that God's word provides for our mature nourishment and enjoyment (Heb 5:11–14). The diet that God's word offers to us is more than enough to meet all our needs at all stages and in all circumstances of our earthly lives, because it provides us with heavenly food that energizes us with the Holy Spirit and gives us a foretaste of all the good things that we will enjoy forever with God in heaven (Heb 6:4–5).

I n his First Letter to Timothy, Paul urges him to teach the congregation in Ephesus that marriage and food are good gifts of God that are to be "received with thanksgiving" and "sanctified by God's word and by prayer" (4:1–6 NRSV). By teaching this, he will be a good minister of Jesus Christ and show his congregation that he is "nourished on the words of the faith and of the good teaching," which he himself has followed in teaching them about their enjoyment of marriage and food. The words of the gospel that he teaches his congregation nourish him in his ministry as they nourish them in their faith.

Since God's word nourishes its hearers, it is spiritually healthy. Like wholesome food, it produces good health for those who assimilate it. This is what Paul explores in his pastoral letters to Timothy and Titus by his use of the Greek participle for "being healthy," which is usually translated in English as an adjective, "sound," an archaic term for healthy that is now largely misunderstood as "correct" or "reasonable."

In 1 Timothy 6:3–4, Paul says, "Whoever teaches what is false and does not agree with the healthy words of our Lord Jesus Christ and the teaching that accords with godly piety is puffed up, understanding nothing, but is sick with controversy and disputes about words." The words of Jesus promote the teaching that accords with the practice of piety. They protect people from the spiritual sickness that infects them in their being and thinking and interactions with others (6:4–5). Thus, "the healthy words of our Lord Jesus Christ" are the source of spiritual health for the whole life of every Christian.

The healthy words of Jesus that nourish personal health also result in healthy teaching that distinguishes the message of the gospel from the observance of the Ten Commandments (1 Tim 1:8–11). It produces "love that issues from a pure heart and a good conscience and sincere faith" (1:5; see also 2 Tim 1:13). Since that is so, pastors, like Timothy, must hold on to the trustworthy word of God, so that they can provide the healthy instruction that accords with healthy teaching (Titus 1:9; 2:1). They need to do this patiently and persistently, even though their "healthy teaching" will not satisfy those who are driven by their disordered emotions and desires (2 Tim 4:3). The goal of all healthy teaching is that the people who heed it will be "healthy in faith, in love, and in endurance" (Titus 2:2). The healthy words of Jesus make people healthy and keep them healthy.

In John 6:25–58, Jesus teaches that he does not just feed his disciples with his wholesome words; through them he offers himself to them for their nourishment in life-giving words (John 6:63), the words of eternal life (6:68). He is the bread of God, the true bread from heaven that gives life to the world (6:32–33). He is the bread of life (6:35, 48), the life-giving bread from heaven (6:51, 58). He provides his disciples with a meal in which he gives them his flesh to eat and his blood to drink (6:51–58). Those who feed on him in it will never again go hungry and never again be thirsty (6:35). He nourishes us as we feed on him and his word.

# X

# GOD'S WORD HEALS

He sent his word and healed them, and
delivered them from destruction.

*Psalm 107:20 ESV*

**W**e all know how words can heal, words that are wise and kind, apt and helpful. That is most evident when they address what we think and feel about ourselves, and how we relate to others and how they relate to us. The words of a good counselor can mend a broken heart and heal a broken relationship. Just as nasty words damage people badly, wise words can heal the worst hurts.

The power of words to wound and heal is explored at some length and in considerable detail in the book of Proverbs, the book that teaches the wisdom that comes from God for those who respect him and his provision for all people on earth.

There the teacher of wisdom instructs his son, his student, on the power of wise words to heal:

> My son, be attentive to my words;
>> incline your ear to my sayings.
> Let them not escape from your sight;
>> keep them within your heart.
> For they are life to those who find them,
>> and healing to all their flesh.
> Keep your heart with all vigilance,
>> for from it flow the springs of life. (Prov 4:20–23)

The student is urged to take the wise words of his teacher to heart by listening attentively to them and looking for insight from them as they convey vitality and health to him from his heart to his whole being. Like good medicine, the words of wisdom bring life and health from the heart to the whole body (cf. 14:30). Like a spring of water, the outflow of healthy life from his heart into his body depends on the inflow of healthy life into it.

Wise words that are kind and gracious do more than just that. Good words make a sad heart glad (Prov 12:25). Like a honeycomb, they offer something delicious and sweet for the hearer to relish and enjoy and the speaker to provide satisfaction and enjoyment to others (Prov 12:18). So just as the tongue can be used recklessly as a sword to wound and kill, it can also be used wisely to bring healing and health to others (Prov 12:18). In fact, "the tongue that brings healing is a tree of life" (Prov 15:4 NIV84). It is a little like the life-giving tree that

God gave to Adam and Eve in the garden of Eden (Gen 2:9; 3:22, 24). It restores some of the God-given vitality that they and their descendants had lost by their expulsion from Eden.

As the Creator of all people on earth, the living God is the source of their physical life and health on earth. He conveys health to them through their nourishment by food and supplies healing for them through the medical care of doctors, nurses, and health workers. In addition to that, he provides his people with spiritual health, the health of the whole person in body and soul, in mind and in spirit, partially through the words of his prophets and fully through the words of Jesus. Through Jesus he heals them completely from the inside out, from their spirits to their souls to their minds and their bodies. The healing Jesus brings is a lifelong process of convalescence and recovery that begins now with the renewal of their spirits and culminates in the resurrection of their bodies for eternal life with God (Rev 22:16; Titus 3:4–5). Paul refers to that divine work of spiritual re-creation and renewal in this benediction: "May the God of peace himself sanctify you entirely; may your spirit and soul and body be kept completely healthy and blameless at the coming of our Lord Jesus Christ" (1 Thess 5:23).

In the Old Testament, God presented himself to his people as their physician. He said, "I am the LORD, your healer" (Exod 15:28). He promised the people he had rescued from Egypt that if they listened to his voice and kept his commandments, he would not inflict any of the diseases on them that he had unleashed on the Egyptians (see also Exod 23:25–26 and Deut 7:15). Like King Hezekiah (Isa 38:16), they therefore prayed to him for healing (Pss 6:2; 41:4). And he kept his promise to heal them. Since he sent his word to heal them in answer to their cries for help (Ps 107:17–20), they praised him for healing all their diseases (Ps 103:3) and bandaging their broken hearts (Ps 147:3).

But sadly, by 740 BC his people were so completely riddled with sickness from their rebellion against God (Isa 1:2–6) that they refused to heed God's word and rejected his call to repentance (Isa 1:16–20; 5:24). By rejecting his word, they forfeited the healing that they could have received from God (Isa 6:10). So when God called Isaiah to be a prophet, he told Isaiah that his word would have the opposite effect on them (Isa 6:5–10). It would not bring them healing but disclose the lethal outcome of their terminal sickness. The word that Isaiah spoke would make their sickness even worse by increasing their defiance of God and aggravating their refusal to listen to him. They would switch off to him deliberately and completely. His word would therefore make them harden their hearts and minds, shut off their ears, and close their eyes to what God was saying to them and doing with them. By switching off to God, they would lose their capacity to receive God's healing until the sickness had run its full course, and they would be ready to listen once again (Isa 6:11–13).

After that time of sickness, a day of healing would come for God's people in the new city of Zion (Isa 33:13–24). God promised that he himself would come in judgment and deliverance to heal the spirits of his people completely from the guilt of their sin and their rebellion against him (Isa 57:18–19; Jer 30:12–17; 33:6–8). He promised to usher in a new day that would bring righteousness and health to his people, a day when the Sun of righteousness would rise with healing in his wings (Mal 4:2). On that day his people would be healed by the wounds of God's suffering servant, who would bear their sin and guilt and sorrow (Isa 53:5).

That is what Jesus has done. He has healed us by bearing our sins, so that we might die to sin and live to righteousness (1 Pet 2:24). He uses God's word as a scalpel to penetrate deep into our bodies and souls and spirits to perform a kind of open-heart surgery on us (Heb 4:12–13). He operates on us with his word that diagnoses our malady and heals it. He does not just treat the physical symptoms of our sickness but deals with the underlying cause of our infection, our sinful unbelief and mistrust of God. He does not just bring temporary relief from its effects, like remission from cancer; he grants us complete relief and lasting health by the gift of eternal salvation (Heb 5:9).

So just as God had promised to be the healer of the Israelites who kept his laws, Jesus presents himself as a good physician, a different physician with a different people with a different kind of healing (Matt 9:12; Luke 5:31–32). He treats those who are penitent sinners with the medicine of forgiveness and provides them with relief from the deadly, pervasive sickness of sin. That is his divine mission. The context of this mission statement by Jesus is significant. Jesus had healed a paralyzed man by forgiving his sins and telling him to get up on his feet and walk home (Matt 9:1–8; Luke 5:17–26). After this, he called the tax collector

Matthew to follow him and accepted Matthew's invitation to take part in a meal for him in Matthew's house together with a crowd of tax collectors and other guests (Matt 9:10; Luke 5:29). There he responded to the criticism of him by the teachers of the law and the Pharisees for eating and drinking with sinners: "It is not the healthy who need a doctor, but the sick. I have not come to call the righteous but sinners to repentance" (Luke 5:31–32). Jesus was sent by his heavenly Father to provide healing for the radical sickness of all people, healing for self-acknowledged sinners rather than self-righteous people who relied on spiritual self-diagnosis and self-medication for their health. Like the paralyzed man who was brought to Jesus by his friends, sinners like Matthew are unable to walk in the way of God's law to gain and retain health for themselves. So Jesus calls them to repent by following him; he heals their spiritual paralysis by forgiving them.

The inspired singer of Psalm 107 thanks God for sending his word to heal the people who were infected with sickness by their rebellion against God and tormented by their iniquities (107:17–20). This song envisages God's word as a messenger that God had sent to heal people who were sick from sin and rescue them from certain death. In his address to the Roman centurion Cornelius, Peter recalls the words in verse 20 of this psalm to tell him about Jesus (Acts 10:36, 38). God had sent his healing word to the people of Israel by sending Jesus to them and anointing him with the Holy Spirit as the promised Messiah. Through Jesus the Messiah, the Lord of all people on earth, the Lord God himself preached the good news of peace to them as he had promised in Isaiah 52:7. By preaching the gospel, Jesus did good things for them and healed them from oppression by the devil (10:36). Thus Peter associates the proclamation of God's word with healing and deliverance from the devil. Then later Peter connects both of these with the forgiveness of sins that is received by those who believe in Jesus as the Messiah and Lord of all (10:43). These four things— God's word, healing, deliverance, and forgiveness—all belong together as part of a single enactment by God. Healing comes from the proclamation of the gospel by Jesus, who had been anointed by God's Spirit. The gospel brings the divine word of healing because it delivers people from oppression by the devil and offers forgiveness of sins to every believer.

It is therefore not at all surprising that the preaching and teaching of the gospel is correlated with various kinds of healing in the Gospels. Take, for example, the summaries of what Jesus did in Matthew. In 4:23 he reports, "And he [Jesus] went throughout all Galilee, teaching in their synagogues and proclaiming the gospel of the kingdom and healing every kind of disease and affliction among the people." We find the same summary in 9:25 apart from a reference to "all the towns and villages" rather than "all Galilee." Matthew implies that healing accompanies the proclamation of the gospel, because the gospel does not just announce the arrival of God's kingdom but also brings healing to people who hear it and believe in it. Jesus did not just heal the centurion's paralyzed servant with his word (8:8) but also usually healed all kinds of sick and disabled people by what he said to them (8:3; 9:1, 6; 9:2; 12:13). Jesus also used his word to heal people who were haunted and possessed by evil spirits (8:16; 15:28; 17:18). In both cases, his words restored them to health.

It is telling that Matthew not only connects the healing ministry of Jesus with his proclamation of the gospel (4:23) but also lists the five basic diseases that Jesus healed (4:24).

- Ill health from various diseases (8:16; 9:12; 14:35; 17:15)

- Extreme pain (8:6)

- Demonization (8:16, 28; 9:32; 12:22; 15:22)

- Lunacy (17:15)

- Paralysis (8:6; 9:26)

Elsewhere Matthew mentions the healing of other afflictions, disabilities of various kinds.

- Blindness (9:27; 20:29; 21:14)

- Blindness with muteness (12:22)

- Muteness (9:32)

- A withered hand (12:10)

- Lameness (11:5; 21:16)

- Deafness (11:4)

From this we can see that, even though Matthew, like the other evangelists, did distinguish between various kinds of sickness, he understood it more widely than we usually do. For him sickness included physical disability, insanity, and harassment by evil spirits. Jesus healed all of these diseases and afflictions with a word (Matt 8:17). Thereby he fulfilled Isaiah's prophecy about the removal of our illnesses and diseases by the vicarious suffering of the Messiah (Isa 53:4–5).

Since Jesus healed people with his teaching and preaching, it was no wonder that people came from far and near to hear him (Luke 6:17–19). They came to hear him so that they would be healed of their diseases and be cured from the evil spirits that haunted them. They came to hear him because their spiritual health depended on his word. Their faith in him healed them (Matt 9:22; Mark 10:52; Luke 17:19) and saved them from sin (Luke 7:50). The same verb is used by Jesus in all these cases. Jesus made them well by saving them; he saved them by making them well. Like them we too depend on Jesus and his word for our health and safety. He also says to us, "Your faith has made you well" (Matt 9:22; Mark 5:34; Mark 10:52; Luke 8:48; Luke 17:19; Luke 18:42). His saving word makes and keeps us safe and well.

God's word has the power to heal us in body, soul, and spirit. It does not heal us partially and temporally, but completely and eternally. Yet it does not do that all at once on any single occasion. It repeatedly addresses those things that attack our spiritual health and cause various bouts of sickness as they arise in our life on earth. It treats us according to our needs in a lifelong journey of spiritual convalescence. Thus, even though our bodies have been freed from some sickness by a word of healing, we will fall sick again and eventually die from physical sickness and infirmity. Even though our souls have been freed from guilt by a word of forgiveness, we will sin again and suffer the consequences of our iniquity. Even though our spirits have been freed from the devil and other evil spirits by a word of deliverance, we will be attacked by them again for as long as we live on earth. These episodes of sickness and ill health will require further treatment by Jesus. All of them give us a fore-taste and pledge of our final healing with the resurrection of our bodies as Jesus promises in John 5:25: "Truly, truly, I say to you, an hour is coming, and is now here, when the dead will hear the voice of the Son of God, and those who hear it will live."

# THAT, BY PATIENCE AND COMFORT OF YOUR HOLY WORD

# XI

# GOD'S WORD ENERGIZES

The word of God is living and active.

*Hebrews 4:12 ESV*

God the Father has given Jesus all authority in heaven and on earth and has called him to commission his disciples to do what he has been doing, the supernatural work of God here on earth. For them to succeed in this work, they will need to have access to divine power, the same power that he possesses, the power of the Holy Spirit.

But there's a problem. How can Jesus make this power available to them safely so that it cannot be abused, but can only be used to do what is good according to the gracious will of his heavenly Father? After all, as is evident in the case of the devil, the worst abuse of power is the misuse of spiritual power. How can Jesus make his spiritual power available to his disciples so that they do not use it for their self-aggrandizement or the exploitation of others? How does he prevent them from operating dangerously as spiritual lone rangers and religious self-operators? How can he empower them in such a way that they only can use that power to benefit and not harm themselves and others? How can he arrange that they will receive it only as long as they draw on it properly for themselves and others and will lose it, like a fused electrical circuit, as soon as they abuse it? Better still, how could the attempted misappropriation of it even be able, in some circumstances, to change them from abusers to the right recipients of it? The best way to achieve this is for Jesus to provide his power to them only in himself and his word and give them access to it only through faith in him and his word.

In his Farewell Discourse, on the night before his crucifixion, Jesus made this amazing promise to his disciples who had witnessed the seven great miracles that he had performed from the turning of water into wine to the raising of Lazarus: "Truly, truly, I say to you, whoever believes in me will also do the works that I do, because I am going to the Father" (John 14:12). After his ascension, they would join him in doing his Father's work on earth. That would not be, by any means, an easy task. It would, in fact, be impossible for them to do by their own abilities and powers. Yet that is what Jesus would enable them to do as his friends through their faith in him and its exercise in prayer (John 14:10–11; 15:7–8, 14–16).

Because his disciples have faith in Jesus and his words, they are able to work together with Jesus. Through the words Jesus speaks to them, his Father does his works in Jesus and in those who believe in him ( John 14:10–11). So when people ask Jesus what they have to do to perform God's works, Jesus says, "This is the work of God, that you believe in him whom he has sent" ( John 6:29). In speaking about God's work here, Jesus does not just refer to what God requires us to do, our work for him, but also to what he does for us, his work for us. God works faith in us through Jesus, so that by faith we may do the work of God together with Jesus.

The disciples of Jesus depend on Jesus completely in their service of him. Jesus therefore asserts, "Apart from me you can do nothing" ( John 15:5). Just as the branch of a vine can remain alive and fruitful only if it remains attached to its vine stock, so his disciples are able to do what he gives them to do only as long as they remain in union with him. If they do abide in him, they will be able to join him in doing his Father's work. So Paul rightly regards himself and his colleagues in ministry as "God's fellow workers," coworkers with God, people who do not just work for God but also work with him in the cause of the gospel. He also quite rightly urges all his brothers and sisters in faith to "abound in the work of the Lord" (1 Cor 15:58).

The reliance of the disciples on Jesus and his word for them to do what he calls them to do is shown in two exemplary stories about Peter. The first is found in Matthew 14:22–33. There we hear how Jesus came to his storm-tossed disciples at night in a boat on the lake by walking across the water to reach them. In response to the instruction of Jesus for them to take heart and not be afraid, Peter says, "Lord, if it is you, command me to come to you on the water" (14:28). When Jesus tells him to come, Peter leaves the boat, walks across the water, and comes to Jesus. He takes Jesus at his word and does what he as a human being could not otherwise do. He does not depend on his all too little faith but on the word that Jesus spoke to him. That word inspired his faith and enabled him to act.

The other story about Peter is recorded in Luke 5:1–11. There we hear how Jesus was teaching a crowd of people from Peter's fishing boat as they pressed in to hear God's word. At the end of his address, Jesus turns to Peter who had worked hard with his fellow fishermen during the past night without catching any fish. Jesus tells him to launch out into deep water where fish are seldom to be found at night, let alone by day, and to put down his nets into the lake. Then Peter says, "Master, we toiled all night and took nothing. But at your word I will let down the nets" (5:5). Even though Peter is reluctant to accept his unreasonable advice, he takes Jesus at his word and hauls in a huge catch of fish. Peter's reliance on the word of Jesus gives him success in his work, just as it would later give him even greater success as an apostle in using God's word to fish for people (5:10). In both these cases, the ability to do what was, humanly speaking, impractical and even impossible came from his dependence on the powerful word of Jesus.

The author of Hebrews therefore rightly declares that "the word of God is living and active" (4:12). It is active not just in doing what it says but also in energizing those who hear it. It acts on them and acts in them. It is, literally in Greek, "in-working." It is at work in those who hear it. It energizes them. Just as an electric current energizes an electric motor, so God's word enables them to do what they could not otherwise do. Paul uses the same verb to tell how God who was at work to raise Jesus from the dead was also at work in all believers (Eph 1:19), as well as how he worked miracles through his Spirit in those who heard and believed the gospel of Jesus (Gal 5:1–5). He uses the same verb to claim that just as God was at work in the ministry of Peter to the Jews, he was also at work in his ministry as an apostle to the gentiles (Gal 2:8; see also Eph 3:6). He even tells all the members of the church in Philippi to work out their salvation with fear and trembling, because it is God who works in them to will and work for his good pleasure (2:12–13). Like them, God energizes us, so that we not only wish to do what pleases him but also rely on him to energize us in doing his good and gracious will.

God's word is at work in all believers. In the first letter to the church in Thessalonica, Paul and his colleagues thank God for what he did with all its members through his word. First, he, rather oddly, thanks God for their work as believers, the work of faith, love, and patient hope that they did, and God did in them, because the gospel came to them "in power and the Holy Spirit and with full conviction" (1:2–5). The word they received with joy produced faith and love, hope and patience in them; it empowered them with the Holy Spirit so that they were able to endure persecution and spread the gospel far and wide (1:6–8).

Then a little later in the letter they also thank God more specifically with these words: "And we also thank God, constantly for this, that when you received the word of God, which you heard from us, you accepted it not as the word of men, but as it really is, the word of God, which is at work in you believers" (2:13). Even though God's word, the gospel of God (2:2, 9), was proclaimed by human speakers in human language, it had the power to energize people because it was the divine word. It did not energize all people to do God's work, but only those who heard it as his word, received it as from him, accepted it as addressed to them, and believed in it as his word for them.

God's word tells us what God has done and is doing for us. It calls us to work for him and tells us what we are to do for him. But it does not stop there and leave us to our own devices to carry out the work that we have been called to do. It actually empowers us to work with Jesus in his mission to the world. It enables us to pass on the gifts that we receive from him. It energizes us with his Holy Spirit so that we can be hearers and doers of God's energizing word.

In this we are a little like ballet dancers whose bodies are synchronized with the music of the dance. The music of the dance does not just tell them what to do, but actually moves them physically and mentally as they dance. They hear the music physically and mentally by letting it carry them along in their dancing. They learn it by heart with their bodies as they go along with it and surrender themselves to it. They therefore do not separate their hearing from their doing or their doing from their hearing. It is one and the same thing for them. That is how it is with us too, as disciples of Jesus who have been called to listen to him by following him. We are to be hearing doers of his word.

Jesus makes this point rather sharply in his conclusion to the Sermon on the Mount in Matthew 7:24–27 and to his Sermon on Level Ground in Luke 6:17–19. In both these passages, Jesus contrasts those who do his words with those who merely hear them by comparing the doers with a house built on solid rock and the hearers with a house built on shifting sand. Yet this simple parable is all too readily misinterpreted and misapplied in a moralistic way. Jesus does not contrast theological theory with moral practice. He does not call his disciples to the obedience of the law but to the obedience of faith, obedience to God's demands in the light of the gospel. The literal sense of obedience in Hebrew and Greek is listening to what has been said, whether it be a command or a promise. They are to carry out God's word by relying on it to receive what he promises to give them and to do what he requires them to do by the power that it provides. They cannot do what God demands by themselves with their own resources but only by relying on Jesus and his words. In Luke's Gospel Jesus emphasizes this point by contrasting those who come to him, hear his words, and do them with those who hear his words and do not do them (6:47). They do not actually hear them at all.

Jesus and his words provide not merely the initial basis for a life of faith but the enduring foundation for both faith and works. Apart from Christ and his words, people can neither believe in him nor work with him in God's family. Their faithful hearing of his words results in their faithful doing of them. They are two sides of the same coin. Yet the hearing comes first. Then with the hearing comes the doing of it. Just as the proper hearing of God's word includes the understanding of what it says, so it also includes the enactment of it in and by those who believe in it. Jesus makes the same point a little later in Luke's Gospel in connection with his own mother and brothers: "My mother and my brothers are those who hear the word of God and do it" (8:21).

So then, Jesus gives us his word to tell us what to do for him and to empower us to work together with him. This is mentioned quite explicitly in the biblical teaching on prayer and praise.

Jesus has this to say to his disciples about the connection of his words with prayer in John 15:7–8: "If you abide in me, and my words abide in you, ask whatever you wish, and it will be done for you." Jesus commands his disciples to pray for what they want to receive from God and promises that their prayers will be answered. But that is qualified in a surprising way. Their prayers will be answered if they do two things when they pray. First, they need to abide in Jesus and remain united with him, so that he can guide and empower them as they pray. They then will not pray by themselves but will be enabled to pray together with him; they will pray in his name (14:13; 15:16; 16:23–24).

In that way they will join with Jesus in prayer just as he joins with them in prayer.

Second, the words of Jesus need to abide in disciples so that they know what to pray for and are empowered to pray by them. By his commands he tells them to pray and what to pray for; by his promises he tells them what they will receive for themselves and others. By giving them his words, he enables them to pray according to his good and gracious will for all people (15:14–16). If his words remain in them, they will know what he wills and desires. By his words their wills will match his will. When they will what he wills and desire what he desires, they will be able to ask whatever they wish for themselves and others, freely and confidently, and it will be done for them because they pray according to his will (1 John 5:14–15).

In Colossians 3:15, Paul traces the connection between the word of Christ and the song of thanksgiving: "Let the word of Christ dwell in you [plural] richly in all wisdom as you teach and admonish each other in psalms and hymns and spiritual songs, and as you sing with grace and gratitude in your hearts to God." The gospel of Christ evokes communal songs of thanksgiving because it conveys God's grace to his people. When the word of Christ makes its home in a congregation, it produces all kinds of song. Singing the song of Jesus, in turn, embeds his grace in the hearts of its members and inspires gratitude to God. The word of Christ teaches all the singers to sing the song of grace, by which they teach it to each other wisely in all its riches. The song that sings of Jesus as the Messiah fills the hearts of the singers with the grace of God and gratitude to him for his grace. So when the word of Christ dwells in a congregation, that word turns its members into a grateful choir of thanks-givers (3:15, 17).

More generally, God's word does not just energize our prayer and praise; it empowers everything that we do and say (Col 3:18). We do everything in his name and with his word. We baptize with his word (Eph 5:26). We overcome the devil with his word (Eph 6:17; 1 John 2:14). It empowers all that we do. Through his word we do the work of God as he does his work in us and through us.

In his written sermon, his word of encouragement (13:22), the author of Hebrews tells his congregation that God's word is active and effective (4:11). That is why he encourages them to join him in entering into God's great Sabbath, his heavenly time and place of rest (4:1–11). As they gather for worship, they are to rest from their work so that God can do his work in them. They enter that rest by believing in the word that they have heard (4:2–3). Like them, we too enter God's place of rest by listening to his word and believing in it. Instead of working hard to save ourselves and fend for ourselves, we rely on his energetic word for our salvation.

# XII

# THE MINISTRY OF THE WORD

*The one who hears you hears me.*
*Luke 10:16 ESV*

The ministry of Jesus, which began with his baptism, did not end with his ascension. When he ascended he made it quite clear to his apostles that he would be present in the church with his disciples to the close of the age (Matt 28:20). After his ascension he was invisibly present with them in such a way that he was no longer bound by the normal limitations of time and space and matter. In the introduction to the book of Acts, Luke goes one step further. He says, "In my former book, Theophilus, I wrote about all that Jesus *began* to do and teach until the day he was taken up to heaven, after giving instructions through the Holy Spirit to the apostles he had chosen." The key word here is "began." Luke claims that Jesus continues his work in word and deed in and through the community that he established. While in his Gospel, Luke told his readers what Jesus began to do before his exaltation; in the book of Acts, he describes how he continued that work through the fulfillment of his announcement in Luke 24:47 that repentance and the forgiveness of sins would be proclaimed in his name to all the nations, beginning with Jerusalem.

To be sure, Jesus had completed the work of redemption by his death and resurrection. But after that he delivers the benefits that he gained by his sacrifice of atonement to people through the ongoing proclamation of the gospel. The forgiveness that he gained by his sacrificial death is now conveyed to believers through his word of pardon to them (Acts 13:38–39). God not only reconciled the world to himself through the presentation of Jesus as a sin offering for all people but also gave the ministry of reconciliation to Paul and all other ministers of the word (2 Cor 5:18–21). Through them Jesus offers reconciliation to people as a gift from God. By the word of reconciliation that these spokesmen speak, they reconcile people to God. They work together with Jesus to offer God's grace and favor to people, his pardon and approval as well as the gift of salvation and justification to them (2 Cor 6:1–2).

In Ephesians 2:17–18, Paul speaks about the ongoing work of Jesus in an arresting way: "He came and preached peace to you who were far off and peace to those who were near. For through him we both have access in one Spirit to the Father." In actual fact, Apollos and Paul himself came and preached God's peace to the gentiles who were far from God and to the

Jews who were near him (Acts 18:24–19:10). Yet here he claims that through them as his agents and their preaching of the gospel, Jesus came to preach to these people in Ephesus and give them access to the Father in the Spirit by their preaching. They have access to the Father through the word that Jesus preached to them.

In his earthly ministry, Jesus had taught God's word to two audiences, the public audience of any people who were willing to give him a hearing and the more intimate audience of his disciples who had heard his word and believed in him. The word that had created them as a community of faith also built them up and equipped them to work with him in its communication to others (Acts 20:32). That is the focus in this section that explores the role of God's word in the service of worship.

The community that Jesus established by preaching and teaching the gospel of God initially consisted of about 120 believers together with the eleven apostles (Acts 1:12–15). They gathered in a house with a large upper room that belonged to Mary the mother of Mark (Acts 12:2, 12). It may have been the same place where Jesus had given his farewell sermon to his disciples and instituted his Supper with them (Luke 22:12). That community was called a church, the assembly of believers in Jerusalem (Acts 5:11; 8:1, 3, 11). They had been assembled by God through his word for the proclamation of his word. There those who were believers devoted themselves to the teaching of the word by the apostles and the breaking of bread by them as well as the presentation of a communal offering and communal prayer (Acts 2:42). In that mother church and in every other church, the risen Lord Jesus continued and still continues to teach God's word by what he says and what he does.

The story of the appearance of Jesus to the two disciples on the road to Emmaus in Luke 24:13–35 shows us how Jesus continued his ministry in the church after his resurrection. It tells us what happened on the evening of Easter Sunday. These two unnamed disciples had heard about the resurrection of Jesus but did not understand the significance of what they had heard. When Jesus joined them on their journey, they did not at first recognize him. As far as they knew, he was dead and buried. His death was the end of his work and the end of their hope of redemption by him. Then Jesus made himself known to them in two stages. First, he preached himself to them from the Old Testament. He opened the Scriptures for them by showing how, and why, the Christ, the Messiah, had to suffer and die before he entered his glory. Yet, even though their hearts burned with joy as he spoke, they still did not recognize him. Then, when they had invited him to stay overnight with them as their guest, he acted as if he was their host when they sat down for the evening meal. He took the bread, gave thanks, broke it, and gave it to them, just as he had done when he instituted his holy Supper three nights earlier. They recognized him in the breaking of the bread, Luke's term for Holy Communion (Luke 24:35; Acts 2:42, 46; 20:7). As soon as they recognized him, he vanished from their sight.

This story shows us how the risen Lord Jesus ministers to us when we assemble for worship. Each Sunday the risen Lord Jesus, who travels with us through life as our unseen companion, makes himself known to us by word and deed in the divine service. This happens in two stages. First, Jesus uses the word of God from the Old Testament to preach himself as our crucified and risen Lord in the readings of the New Testament and in the sermon that is preached from them. Second, he hosts a meal in which he speaks himself to us and feeds us with his own body and blood.

We discover two things about the preaching of God's word from this dramatic account. First, Jesus himself is the preacher in the church, the assembly of God's people. He is also the sermon; he preaches himself to us in the divine service. By his word that he speaks to us, he offers himself to us. Human preachers are merely his mouthpiece, his spokesmen. He says, "He who listens to you listens to me" (Luke 10:16). If we listen to them, we receive him and the Father who sent him (Matt 10:40).

Second, the preaching of the gospel is closely connected with the Lord's Supper. What Jesus tells us about himself in his word he gives to us through his word in holy Communion. The same Jesus who preaches himself to us in the Gospels and in the sermon offers himself and all his gifts to us there by saying, "Take, eat; this is my body. ... Drink of it [the cup], all of you, for this is my blood of the new covenant, which is poured out for many for the forgiveness of sins" (Matt 26:27–28). There he presents the body and blood that he offered up for us by his death on the cross. So the preaching of the word goes hand in hand with the celebration of the holy meal. In both of these, he does what he says. He teaches himself to us by giving himself and his gifts to us in these two different ways.

From Pentecost onward Jesus was at work in the church that he had created through his word as it was preached and taught by human speakers. The leaders of the church were those who spoke the word of God to its members (Heb 13:7). First came the apostles, like Peter and Paul. Then came those whom they appointed to join with them and succeed them in the ministry of the word (Acts 6:4; 14:23), the ministry of reconciliation (2 Cor 5:18). They were not self-appointed teachers of spirituality but preachers whom God had commissioned to preach the gospel, the word of Christ (Rom 10:14–17), the word of God's grace (Acts 14:3; 20:24). As servants of Christ they were servants of the word (Luke 1:2; 1 Cor 4:1). They assisted him with the proclamation of his word. Yet they did not do this by themselves, apart from him, but in union with him and in the presence of God the Father (2 Cor 2:17; 12:19). They did not rely on their eloquence and persuasive power, but on the power of the Holy Spirit, so that the faith of their hearers would not depend on them but on Jesus and the power of his Holy Spirit (1 Cor 2:4–5; 1 Thess 1:4–5). Their basic task was to preach the word to their members and use it in their teaching to convince, correct, and encourage them (2 Tim 4:1–3).

They preached and taught God's word in the assembly of God's people, the congregation where Jesus was present with his disciples (Matt 18:20). We get an incidental description of such an assembly in Troas (Acts 20:7–12). That congregation assembled on Sunday evening to listen to Paul's address and celebrate the Lord's Supper. God's word was spoken to the congregation in the reading of the Scriptures and the proclamation of the gospel from them. Because the New Testament did not exist until much later, the apostles and teachers in the early church followed the practice of the synagogue with one or two readings from the Pentateuch and Prophets. After the congregation had heard these readings, the teacher would use them to teach the gospel as Jesus had done in the synagogue at Nazareth (Luke 4:16–21) and Paul did in the synagogue at Antioch in Pisidia (Acts 13:14–41). In their preaching they used the words and stories of Jesus to proclaim the gospel to their hearers.

In 1 Corinthians 4:1, Paul describes himself and Sosthenes as "servants of Christ and stewards of the mysteries of God." That does not just apply to him; it applies to every minister of the word. They are stewards of God's mysteries. By their preaching they proclaim the mystery of Christ in the church. They do not speak for an absent Christ; they speak for Christ who stands among them and is invisibly present with them.

S ome years ago I saw a rather gripping Australian film called *The Last Wave*. It was set in Sydney and told the story of an irreligious, secular, well-educated young man who had become aware of the supernatural realm by his association with a group of urban Aborigines in Sydney. In the middle of the film, he visits his stepfather, an Anglican priest, and unsuccessfully seeks help from him in making sense of what he has experienced. In exasperation he says to the hapless man, "Dad, you never told me that there were any mysteries." Indignant, his stepfather replies, "That's not true! I've tried to explain the mysteries of Christianity to you again and again." At this his son exclaims, "You never explained them, Dad; you explained them away!"

Like many modern people, we tend to confuse mysteries with secrets. And so we explain them away. But a mystery is different from a secret. Even though both have to do with something that is hidden and unknown, a mystery differs from a secret in one important respect. A secret remains a secret only as long as you don't know it. Once it is revealed, it ceases to be a secret. But a mystery remains a mystery even when it is revealed. In fact, the more you know about it, the more mysterious it becomes. Take, for example, the mystery of life or of love. You may be able to explain some things about them, but you can never really explain what they are. Any explanation, no matter how accurate it may be, is always like a sketch of a person with pencil on paper, a poor substitute for the real thing.

In his explanation of the parable of the sower, Christ says that the mysteries of God are revealed through the proclamation of the word (Mark 4:11; cf. Matt 13:11; Luke 8:10). After Jesus has taught this parable to the crowd, the twelve apostles and his other disciples ask him to explain this parable to them. He then tells them that the mystery of God's kingdom has been given only to them; it is inaccessible to those who are outside his circle of disciples, even though they see what he does and hear what he says.

In Mark's Gospel, Jesus has five main things to say about the mystery of God's kingdom, his eventual rule over the whole of his creation (Mark 4:1–25). First, God's gracious rule on earth is concealed from human sight and yet revealed in Jesus the Messiah. In his humanity, Jesus embodies the mystery of God's kingdom. He ushers in God's kingdom, mysteriously, by his incarnation, teaching, and sacrificial death. Like his identity as God's Son, the Messiah, his kingdom is not apparent to human perception. Paradoxically, that mystery is concealed in his humanity in order to be revealed in a hidden way by his teaching in parables (4:11–12). His word reveals what is otherwise hidden from human perception (4:22).

Second, God reveals the mystery of his kingdom through his word, the word that Jesus preaches and teaches. The use of theological passive formula "it has been given" indicates that God the Father gives the disciples access to it (4:11). Jesus is the sower of the seed, the word of God that produces repentance and speaks forgiveness to those who receive it.

Third, only his disciples have access to this mystery (4:11). This is rather surprising, for the word that reveals this mystery is preached to all comers. Yet Jesus explains the word only to his disciples who have faith in him (4:1, 10–13, 33–34). He initiates them into the mystery of God's kingdom. They alone have ears to hear the mystery (4:9, 23), because the mystery is always a divine gift that can only be had as it is received through hearing God's word. It comes to the disciples of Jesus through hearing his word rather than their observation of him and what he does.

Fourth, the word that reveals the mystery is like a lamp that lights up a one-room ancient Palestinian house at night (4:21–23). The preaching of the gospel is a theophany, the Father's self-disclosure to his royal sons, a divine self-manifestation that illumines and enlightens the disciples of Jesus. It produces the harvest of light in them. By his preaching, Jesus discloses the hidden mysteries of God's kingdom verbally rather than visually. Its manifestation is like the theophanies in the Old Testament. Unlike pagan theophanies in which deities showed their faces visibly to their devotees for replication in the idols that gave ongoing access to them, the Lord appeared to the Israelites at Sinai by speaking to them and by his name that was spoken to them with the Aaronic benediction in the divine service. So, too, in this age, Jesus discloses God's hidden presence by what he says to his disciples.

In Mark, Jesus speaks about the mystery (singular) of God's kingdom because Mark wants to emphasize its embodiment in Jesus; in Matthew and Luke he speaks about the knowledge of its mysteries (plural). Their focus is on their human appropriation of God's manifold gifts by the reception of Christ and his teachings.

Matthew puts the emphasis on understanding the word (13:13, 14, 15, 19, 23). He omits the parable of the lamp, apart from its interpretative sentences about the abundance of gifts for those who are enlightened. This is added to the words of Jesus to his disciples about God's gift of knowledge to them (13:12), the knowledge that leads to repentance and divine healing (13:15). He also adds the words of congratulation by Jesus to his disciples for seeing and hearing what all the prophets had longed for so ardently (13:16–17). So, in Matthew the people who understand the word of the kingdom produce the varied harvest of spiritual health according to their level of understanding. Theophany comes through spiritual understanding, insight into the mysteries of God's hidden rule through Jesus, the Messianic King.

Like Matthew, Luke puts the emphasis on the knowledge of the mysteries of God's kingdom that comes from hearing the word. On the one hand, he stresses the role of the church as the place for divine theophany by adding the clause "so those who come in can see the light" (Luke 8:16). He seems to envisage the house churches where the gospel was preached in his day. The enlightening word lights up each congregation and shines out from it into the world of darkness. The proclamation of the gospel therefore draws those who are outside the church into it and the light of Christ. On the other hand, instead of focusing on *what* is heard, as in Mark and Matthew, Jesus speaks in

Luke about *how* the word of God is heard (8:18). It needs to be retained for it to produce saving faith (8:12) and the harvest of enlightenment (8:16–18). Only those who keep on hearing the word with a good and honest heart and retain it there through meditation on it receive the gift of knowledge, the practical, experiential knowledge of God's mysteries, for the word alone gives continual access to them. So, in Luke the word of God initiates the disciples into the mysteries of God's kingdom by giving the knowledge of salvation and the enlightenment that comes from the persistent retention of the illuminating word in their hearts. The gospel lights up the circle of Christ's disciples, shines out from them into the world, and attracts people from its darkness to the light of God's presence. The church therefore is the place for theophany, the place where divine mysteries are revealed through the proclamation of God's word.

When the word of God is preached in the divine service, the congregation has access to the mystery of Christ. Paul speaks about his disclosure of it in this way in Colossians 1:25–27: "I became a minister [of the church] according to the stewardship from God that was given me for you, to fully proclaim the word of God, the mystery hidden for ages and generations but now revealed to his saints. To them God chose to make known how great among the gentiles are the riches of the glory of this mystery, which is Christ among you, the hope of glory." Here the apostle Paul depicts himself as the steward of a mystery. That mystery is the hidden presence of the risen, glorified Lord Jesus with his people in the church. Paul discloses the mystery of his real presence to the saints, those who are united with Christ and so share in his holiness. Paul reveals the hidden presence and activity of the risen Lord to them by preaching God's word to them, the gospel that proclaims Christ and brings "life and immortality to light" for its hearers (2 Tim 1:10). He uses the prophetic Scriptures of the Old Testament to preach the mystery of Christ (Rom 16:25–26).

Apart from God's word, we have no access to the risen Lord Jesus; we have no knowledge or experience of him. That word proclaims Christ's presence to us and introduces him to us. It initiates us into the mystery of Christ, something that no eye has seen, no ear has heard, and no human heart has ever conceived (1 Cor 2:6–10). The disclosure of his hidden presence gives us a glimpse of glory here on earth. We have access to the mystery of Christ in a most unlikely place and in a most unlikely way—in the church that has been gathered for worship and through the proclamation of God's word by human preachers in that congregational assembly.

# WE MAY EMBRACE AND EVER HOLD FAST THE BLESSED HOPE OF EVERLASTING LIFE

# XIII

# GOD'S WRITTEN WORD

> Whatever was written in former days was
> written for our instruction, that through
> endurance and through the encouragement
> of the Scriptures we might have hope.
>
> *Romans 15:4 ESV*

God's word is living and active. It is not meant to be archived in a written text for academic analysis and the discovery of spiritual principles and ideas about God and his relationship with us; it is meant to be spoken face-to-face, from the mouth of a speaker into the ears and hearts of its hearers for faith in their salvation and their encouragement in hope. Yet, surprisingly, that is why it has been written in what we now call the Bible. The spoken word has been written to aid and safeguard its oral communication. It therefore comes into its own as a text for preaching and teaching. The written word does not replace the spoken word but enables it to be handed down through the ages, so that it is spoken and heard from generation to generation. That is so for both parts of the Bible.

Consider the Old Testament. God's word that had been spoken to the Israelites for a particular purpose at a particular time and place was written down so that it could be spoken and heard by his people in another context or, even, in every context. Its written form helped to extend God's word beyond its original audience to a new audience as well as to his people at all times and in all places. Thus the words of God about his day of judgment for the Northern Kingdom through Amos were collated and edited so that they would apply to God's day of judgment for Judah and his final day of judgment for his people on earth. These written works were called "the Scriptures," a term which means that they had been written down to be read, studied, and reapplied. Then after God's words had been written down to pass them on to future generations, some of these Scriptures were gathered together with other similar material and combined in a single scroll, like the twelve Minor Prophets from Hosea to Malachi. As well as that, they were all eventually, by the time of Jesus, collated in three parts and listed according to their liturgical authority and their use in teaching—"the Law," "the Prophets," and "the Writings" (which was also called the Psalms from its first scroll in Luke 24:44).

The five scrolls of the Law were associated with Moses and used by the priests to regulate the service of worship at the temple in Jerusalem (Ezra 3:2–5; 1 Chron 6:49). They were also used to train new priests on how to conduct the divine service and to instruct the Israelites about their right participation in it and their right behavior in keeping with God's will for them as his holy people.

In the Hebrew Bible, the twenty-one works of the Prophets were combined in two parts, the histories of the six "Former Prophets" from Joshua to 2 Kings and the fifteen "Latter Prophets" from Isaiah to Malachi. They were authorized for use together with the Law in the synagogue and were set to be read on the Sabbath. The two readings from the Law and the Prophets were followed by an address that was usually based on the reading from the Law, because the oral exposition of God's word was meant to instruct the congregation in obedience to God's commandments.

The third category of the Hebrew Scriptures was the Writings. Its thirteen written works were not authorized for regular reading and instruction in the synagogue. Their use varied. The Psalms were chanted in the temple and the synagogue. The five "Festive Scrolls" that consisted of the Song of Songs, Ruth, Lamentations, Ecclesiastes, and Esther were read in the synagogue on annual commemorations. Proverbs, Job, and Daniel as well as Ezra, Nehemiah, and Chronicles were, most likely, used only for study and educational purposes.

I n sum: The Old Testament Scriptures were a collection of writings that codified the word that God had spoken to his people through his prophets from Noah to Moses, from Samuel to Malachi, from David to Solomon. They were regarded as prophets because they had been chosen by God to hear his word and inspired by his Spirit to speak it to others (1 Tim 3:16; 2 Pet 1:21). They were meant to teach God's word to his people. That includes us who belong to his eschatological community (Heb 1:2), the earthly assembly of people who have unrestricted access to his presence through Jesus, our great high priest (Heb 4:6; 10:19–22; 12:22–24).

There was no New Testament in the early church until the third century AD. But there was much preaching and teaching of God's word. From the beginning, Jesus and the apostles used the Scriptures of the Old Testament in their proclamation of the gospel. They based what they said on them. But even in the time of Jesus, there was no single Hebrew or Greek Bible; rather, there were thirty-nine different writings of various sizes. They were not written on paper in books with pages but on leather parchment in scrolls (Luke 4:17). The Scriptures were also called by other names in the books that now make up the New Testament—"Scripture" (1 Tim 4:16; 2 Pet 1:20), "the Law"—in the Hebrew sense of divine instruction (John 10:24; Rom 3:19; 1 Cor 14:21), or, quite commonly, "the Law and the Prophets," because these parts were read and used for instruction in the synagogue and the church (Matt 7:12; 22:40; Luke 16:16; Acts 28:23). These works were the Scriptures, the Bible of the apostles and the preachers in the early church. They adhered to this axiom in their preaching and teaching: "Do not go beyond what is written" (1 Cor 4:6). Their word had to be consistent with the Scriptures.

The Old Testament was the Bible of Jesus. He regarded it as the word of his heavenly Father (John 10:35) and used it to preach himself (Luke 24:21). He claimed that the Scriptures bore prophetic witness to him (John 5:39–42, 46; cf. Luke 24:44); by themselves they did not give eternal life; rather, they directed their readers to seek and receive it through faith in him (John 5:39–40). Jesus also taught that he had not come to abolish them but to fulfil them entirely by his life, death, and resurrection (Matt 5:17–18; Luke 16:17).

The Old Testament was also the Bible of the apostles and preachers in the early church. Luke shows how this was so in Acts. He begins this book in 2:14–36 with Peter's sermon on the day of Pentecost with his use of Joel 2:16–21, Psalm 16:8–11, and Psalm 110:1 to preach Jesus as Lord and Christ, and he completes the book with Paul's meeting in 28:17–28 with the Jews in Rome, where he preached Jesus to them from the Law and the Prophets and warned those who refused to believe the gospel with Isaiah 6:9–10. The proclamation of the apostles is summed up best by these words of Paul: "We tell you the good news: What God promised to our fathers, he has fulfilled for us, their children, by raising up Jesus" (Acts 13:32).

All this shaped the pattern of worship in the churches and determined its content. As far as we can gather, people who believed in Jesus as God's Son assembled on Sunday evening to meet with their risen Lord. They assembled to hear the gospel of Jesus and celebrate a holy meal with him as their host (Acts 20:7–11). In that congregational assembly, one or two passages were read from the Old Testament by the leader of the congregation, as was the case in the synagogue. The leader then used those readings to preach the gospel of Jesus and teach God's word to them. Paul refers to this practice in his charge to Timothy as the pastor of the church in Ephesus: "Until I come, devote yourself to the public reading of Scripture, to preaching and to teaching" (1 Tim 4:13 NIV).

We get some idea of how this was done from Paul's sermon in Acts 13:14–41. First, Paul retells the story of God's dealings with the people of Israel from his call of Abraham to his choice of David as a king after his heart to do his will, in order to announce that Jesus, a descendant of David, is the Savior that God has promised, the King who has brought God's salvation to his people (13:17–26). Then Paul moves on to the story of the salvation that God has brought to them through Jesus (13:27–41). As he speaks of the death and resurrection of Jesus, he uses three prophecies from the Old Testament to preach the gospel to them—the prophecy in Psalm 2:7 with God's acknowledgment of the Messiah as his Son; the prophecy in Isaiah 55:3 with God's promise to extend the blessings of his covenant with David to them through his royal Son; and the prophecy of David in Psalm 16:10 with the declaration that God would not allow the body of the Messiah to decay. From this

Paul concludes that those who believe in Jesus as their Savior will receive the forgiveness of sins from him. Then Paul ends the sermon by warning his hearers about the dire consequences of unbelief with God's word to his people in Habakkuk 1:5. Even though we do not know what the readings from the Scriptures were on that Sabbath, we can see how Paul's proclamation of the gospel revolved around two things—the whole of the Old Testament and its fulfillment by Jesus. The whole Old Testament and the gospel of Jesus were equally authoritative for him.

This use of the Old Testament to preach Jesus in the church is also shown by the frequent quotations from it in the New Testament. They are usually introduced by the stock formula "It is written." They mark the words that provide the foundation from the Old Testament for what is preached and taught. It is, however, all too easy to mistake the function of these quotations. They are not meant to win an argument as in a debate with an opponent or prove a legal judgment as in a court of law. They are not meant to prove that the teacher who cites them is right or that those who oppose him are wrong. Rather, they shift the conversation from human words to God's word, from human teaching to God's teaching. They base what is taught on God's wisdom and authority rather than human authority and knowledge. Thus the use of this formula refers an issue back to God and relies on his word for adjudication and agreement.

The function of the formula for quotation from the Old Testament is evident in its use by Jesus. His use of it is rather surprising because he so often speaks with his own right rather than with scriptural authority. In contrast with the teachers of the law, he declares, "I say to you" (Matt 5:22, 26, 32, 34, 43). When he quotes a passage from the Old Testament, he does so for one of three reasons: to announce the fulfillment of a prophecy (Matt 11:10; 26:31), to claim divine authority for what he does (Matt 21:13; Mark 7:6), or to defeat the devil (Matt 4:4, 7, 10). The last use is most telling. He does not quote Scripture to win an argument with the devil, who actually initiates the argument and matches him in that game, but to assert the authority of his heavenly Father and use divine power to vanquish the devil (Matt 4:1–11).

Like Jesus, the apostles and preachers in the early church used the Scriptures to exercise divine power, the power of the Holy Spirit. They held that they were written for the practical instruction of believers. By the words of God that they reported, they encouraged them to trust in Jesus and put their hope in him (John 5:39–40; Rom 15:4). By the acts of God that they recounted, they instructed them positively about what God had done for their salvation and negatively about the peril of disobedience (1 Cor 10:1–12). Thus Paul claims that the Old Testament was written for the instruction of God's people in the church (1 Cor 10:1–12). Above all else, these sacred writings were meant to make every believer "wise for salvation through faith in Jesus Christ" (2 Tim 3:16).

The oral teachings of Jesus and his apostles were eventually written down and gathered together in the books that now make up the New Testament. To be sure, some of these books, such as the letters of the apostles, were written right from the beginning of their existence. Even so, not only was the material in them shaped by oral teaching, but most were meant to be read as a sermon in a congregation. Some of the letters were addressed to a particular church, such as 1 and 2 Corinthians, or group of churches in a particular place, such as Romans. Others were published as circular letters for a number of churches, such as James and 1 Peter. The letters of Timothy and Titus were written to instruct preachers in their pastoral work. As time passed, they were circulated more widely for general use across the church. Finally, by the end of the second century, a general consensus was reached on which of these works was to be regarded as God's word. They were formally authorized to be read together with the Old Testament in congregational worship and used for preaching and teaching in it. They were then brought together for that purpose in a single book, which we now call the New Testament.

The primary purpose of the written New Testament was for use in congregational worship. Yet it was also used in the catechetical instruction of candidates for baptism, the training of pastors and pastoral assistants, and the defense of the Christian faith against false teachers and its critics. Yet because a complete copy of the New Testament—let alone the Old Testament—was so expensive, it was seldom owned and read by individuals.

Most members of the church only heard it as it was read and expounded in the divine service. Thus God's word was usually communicated orally, as it still is even now.

H ere are five ways the Bible still shapes the life of the church. First, the whole of it serves the same purpose as John's Gospel. In 20:31, he states that it was written so that its hearers would believe that Jesus is the Christ, the Son of God, and have life in him through their faith in him. It is, above all else, a book of faith. Through the testimony of the Scriptures, God the Father answers the prayer of Jesus that those who believe in him through the word of his apostles may be one in faith with him, as he is with the Father and the Father is with him, so that the world may believe that the Father has sent him (John 17:20–21).

Second, the Bible is read as God's word in congregational worship. That is where it comes into its own. That is where it belongs. While the choice of what is read in a particular service differs across the churches, the practice of many churches in the English-speaking world is that there is a three-year cycle of three readings, with the first from the Old Testament or Acts with a corresponding psalm in response to it, the second from the letters of the apostles, and the third from the four Gospels. The range of readings is meant to cover "the whole counsel of God" (Acts 20:27).

Third, the proclamation and instruction that is given in the sermon after the readings are based on one or all of them. In their address to the congregation, preachers are not meant to share their own ideas and talk about their own experiences but to preach the gospel of Jesus and apply God's word to the life of the congregation and its members. They have been appointed to do this because the divine power and spiritual effect of their proclamation depends on their faithfulness to God's word.

Fourth, the words of Jesus and his disciples determine what is said and done in the divine service. Thus the gospel is preached and heard, people are baptized and instructed in the Christian faith, sins are confessed and pardoned, prayers are offered to God the Father in the name of Jesus, and the Lord's Supper is celebrated, because Jesus has said that these things are to be done. What's more, everything that is done in the congregation is done with God's word because God's word is meant to be at work in everything that is done. It empowers all that is done with the Holy Spirit.

Fifth, the devotional life of Christians in their homes is shaped by God's word. It revolves around the reading of the Bible as God's word, meditation on it for their spiritual enrichment, and guidance by it in prayer. In that way, the life of every disciple and every household is sanctified by the word of God and prayer (1 Tim 4:5). By Christians' devotion to God's word, God the Father and God the Son come to stay with them (John 14:23).

All this is summed up best by Paul's conclusion for his Letter to the Romans: "Now to him who is able to establish you by my gospel and the proclamation of Jesus Christ, according to the revelation of the mystery hidden for long ages past, but now revealed and made known through the prophetic writings by the command of the eternal God, so that all nations might believe and obey him—to the only wise God be glory forever through Jesus Christ! Amen" (16:25–27 NIV84).

# XIV

# GOD'S AMAZING WORD

### What is this word?
*Luke 4:36 ESV*

e conclude where we began. A large table has been spread before us with many dishes and much more food than any one of us could ever eat in one sitting, let alone even in a whole lifetime. A smorgasbord is set out for the nourishment of everyone in every stage of life and in every situation. Some of it may appeal to me. Some of it, I must admit, may not suit my all too limited and untutored taste. And much of it, sadly, may even repel me. Where then should I begin?

If I begin with what appeals to me, like the teaching on God's love, I may merely confirm my spiritual blindness, entrench my unbelief, and never experience the transformation that leads me into its full riches. It may therefore be better to begin with the things that offend and repel me, like the teaching on

God's wrath against sin, because that would reveal my blind spots and the obstacles that hamper my spiritual reception and growth. Even so, I would not advise anyone to begin there. That would be my counsel for spiritual maturity. So where do I begin? Where do we begin? Yet begin we must, because food is meant to be eaten, and we need the right spiritual nourishment to survive and flourish.

The Bible is not a single book that provides us with nothing more than one or two courses. It is a library of sixty-six books written by many different human authors in different genres for different people at different times and in many different places. A cursory survey of it will not find a single narrative in it with a single plot and a single purpose. Most of its readers find it hard to make sense of the whole. So they pick from it and choose what is congenial to them. Yet the church holds that the whole of the Bible is the word of God for us and all people. It quite rightly assumes that the profusion of material in the Bible has amazing coherence and mysterious unity for the people of God who hear it as his word and receive what he has to give to them in it. But I cannot take all that in at once.

So where are we meant to start with it, and how? The answer is given by the Bible itself, which is confirmed by the church throughout the ages with its confession of faith in Jesus as God's Son in the Apostles' and Nicene Creeds. We are meant to start with the risen Lord Jesus and his words, for it is he, and he alone, who can open the Scriptures to us as he did for his disciples after his resurrection (Luke 24:44–47). We are also meant to approach it as his disciples, his students who listen attentively to him as our teacher and humbly learn from him by living with him. Like Mary, we are to sit at his feet and listen to his word for us (Luke 10:39). We may, indeed, make some sense of the Bible intellectually apart from Jesus and faith in him. But we can only receive what it has to offer to us and do for us through faith in him and his word. Yet that is not just the place to start; it is the place where we are meant to remain, for we can only remain his disciples if we remain in his word (John 8:31).

We can see how this happens from Luke's juxtaposition of two stories in 4:16–36. They describe the effect of his words on two Sabbath days in two different places, first the synagogue in Nazareth, his hometown, and then the synagogue in Capernaum. The setting of both these stories is significant theologically and pastorally. In both places, Jesus teaches God's holy word to his people at a holy time and in a holy service at a holy place. Yet his teaching has a completely different effect. In both cases, the people who hear him are amazed at him. But in the first instance, it leads to their rejection of him and his authority, whereas in the second instance, it results in the acceptance of him and his authority.

In Nazareth, Jesus read the prophecy from Isaiah 61:1–2 in which the Messiah speaks about himself and his divine mission. Then he announced that this prophecy was fulfilled for the people in the synagogue as they heard what Jesus had to say. They heard his gracious words, but they did not receive them as good news for them, God's word of grace to them. Even though they were amazed at his eloquence, they did not really hear what he had to say. So they asked the wrong question about Jesus rather than the right question about his word. They said, "Is not this Joseph's son?" This was not really a question at all, because it assumed the answer. They fancied that they knew Jesus because he was only one of them. They therefore rejected his authority because they held that his words were nothing more than the all too human words of a man who was nothing more than Joseph's son. They dismissed his words by dismissing him and his authority. Since Jesus realized that their question came from their dismissive attitude to him, he issued a scathing critique of his prejudiced critics. He told them that, unlike the widow of Zarephath and Naaman the leper, they would not be cleansed by God and fed by him, because they had refused to accept him as the Messiah. This infuriated them so much that they drove him out of their town and planned to kill him.

As in Nazareth, Jesus also taught God's word to the people in Capernaum. This is what happened there:

And he [Jesus] went down to Capernaum, a city of Galilee. And he was teaching them on the Sabbath, and they were astonished at his teaching, for his word possessed authority. And in the synagogue there was a man who had the spirit of an unclean demon, and he cried out with a loud voice, "Ha! What have you to do with us,

Jesus of Nazareth? Have you come to destroy us? I know who you are—the Holy One of God." But Jesus rebuked him, saying, "Be silent and come out of him!" And when the demon had thrown him down in their midst, he came out of him, having done him no harm. And they were all amazed and said to one another, "What is this word? For with authority and power he commands the unclean spirits, and they come out!" (Luke 4:31–36)

In Capernaum, the people listened to the teaching of Jesus and accepted his authority. They were so astonished at what he said and did that they asked the right question: "What is this word?" And that opened up the right discussion about the authority of Jesus and the power of his word. It too is the question that I would like to consider now.

Well, what is this word? It is, most obviously, the word of Jesus of Nazareth. It is the word of a man who lived a human life on earth from his conception in Mary's womb to his burial in the tomb provided by Joseph of Arimathea. Yet for all that he was no ordinary man. Joseph was not his genetic father, and Nazareth was not his true home. He was not just a man but so much more than a mere man. That was evident in what he said about himself and God. All that he said and did disclosed his true identity.

What then is the word of this man, Jesus? Even though the people in Capernaum did not know who he really was, the spirit of an unclean demon in a man did because he was not distracted by his humanity and was able to discern his spiritual status. That spirit knew whom he had encountered. Like the other demons later in Luke's Gospel (4:41; 8:28), he knew who Jesus was. So he said, "Ha! What have you to do with us, Jesus of Nazareth? Have you come to destroy us? I know who you are—the Holy One of God." God the Father had anointed Jesus with the Holy Spirit in his baptism (Luke 3:21–22; Acts 10:36). He was the Messiah, the Christ, God's anointed priest and king. Since he was also God's Son, Jesus shared his Father's holiness. So, since Jesus was the Holy One of God, his words were holy. They were the holy words of God the holy Father. His holy words exposed the impurity of the unclean spirit and expelled it from the man in the synagogue. The word of Jesus was the word of God's Holy One.

What then is the word of Jesus, the Holy One of God? It is the word that has divine authority, the human word of Jesus that is spoken with God's authority. That was what astonished the people in the synagogue. They were not astonished at the eloquence of his teaching but at its authority. They realized that "his word possessed authority" (Luke 4:32). He did not address them as a prophet who reported what God had said. He did not address them as a teacher of the law who told them what was written in the Old Testament. He spoke with a divine voice. He did not speak as if he were God, but he spoke as God's Son. He spoke God's word to them directly by saying, "I say to you." So the people in Capernaum realized that Jesus spoke God's word to them with divine authority that required them to listen to it as his disciples.

What is the word that Jesus speaks with authority as the Holy One of God? It is the word of divine power, the power of the Holy Spirit. That word therefore had supernatural power, the power to silence demons and drive them from the people they possessed, the power to disempower and destroy them. So Jesus did not engage in battle for power with them but merely spoke two commands to them as his underlings: "Be silent and come out of him." He addressed the spirit like a dog with rabies and said, "Be muzzled!" Those words did what Jesus commanded; they silenced the spirit and expelled it from the man. The people in the synagogue were so astonished by the authority and power of his words that they asked each other and us, "What is this word? For with authority and power he commands the unclean spirits, and they come out."

What is the word that Jesus speaks to them and to us with divine authority and power? It is the word that amazes those who hear it (Luke 4:32). It amazes them with what it says and does, things that are extraordinary, things that go beyond normal human experience and confound our normal understanding of life, things that are, in a sense, out of this world, like the deliverance of people from a demon (4:36; 9:43), the healing of a paralyzed man (5:25), the calming of a storm on the lake (8:25), the resuscitation of a dead girl (8:56), the healing of a mute man (11:14), and the appearance of the risen Christ physically to show himself to his disciples on Easter Sunday evening (24:36–43). The amazing thing about these amazing acts is that Jesus does them with his word. His word arouses a sense of awe and wonder in those who listen to Jesus and put their faith in him. His authority and power disarm our independent unbelief and change us into amazed disciples who depend on him completely for our deliverance and have everything to learn from him.

Yet all too often the words of Jesus do not amaze us. We are put off by them because they seem to be too unfamiliar and extraordinary to be believed, or else we become bored with them because they are so familiar and ordinary. I must admit that even though they have so often surprised me and amazed me again and again, I too have at times been put off by them and bored with them. Yet they have also caught me out repeatedly and surprised me once again by what they say and give to me. In fact, my greatest joy and delight has been that I have been called to be a minister of the gospel and a teacher of the Bible. That has confounded all my expectations and led me from amazement to ever greater amazement in my vocation and my unlikely journey with Jesus in which he has taught me to look for what is unexpected in his inexhaustible word.

But I have also been grieved beyond measure at the apparent rejection of God's amazing word by so many of the people that I have known and taught. Their apostasy seems to belie the power of Jesus and his word. All too often his word seems to produce unbelief rather than faith in Jesus. They are like the many disciples who could not stomach what Jesus had to say about himself as the Bread of Life and the gift of his flesh and blood as food and drink for the reception of eternal life; they rejected this hard word of Jesus, turned away from him, and no longer followed him (John 6:60, 66). Yet for all that, Jesus still calls them and me to return to him. He still says, "Whoever comes to me I will never cast out" (6:37).

When I have been disappointed with the people who seem to have fallen away, Jesus has put the same surprising question to me that he put to Peter and the other apostles: "Do you want to go away as well?" I have joined Peter and all the church with his answer to that searching question (John 6:68–69): "Lord, to whom shall we go? You have the words of eternal life, and we have believed, and have come to know, that you are the Holy One of God."

# THROUGH JESUS CHRIST, OUR LORD.
# AMEN.

# NOTES

1. Origen, *Commentary on the Gospel of John* 1.10.
2. Martin Luther, "A Brief Instruction on What to Look For and Expect in the Gospels," in *Church Postil*, LW 35:121; see also LW 75:10.

# SCRIPTURE INDEX

## Old Testament

## New Testament

The Christian Essentials series is
set in TEN OLDSTYLE, designed by
Robert Slimbach in 2017. This
typeface is inspired by Italian
humanist and Japanese
calligraphy, blending
energetic formality
with fanciful
elegance.

# CHRISTIAN ESSENTIALS

*The Christian Essentials series passes down tradition that matters. The ancient church was founded on basic biblical teachings and practices like the Ten Commandments, baptism, the Apostles' Creed, the Lord's Supper, the Lord's Prayer, and corporate worship. These basics of the Christian life have sustained and nurtured every generation of the faithful—from the apostles to today. The books in the Christian Essentials series open up the meaning of the foundations of our faith.*

LEXHAM PRESS

For more information, visit
LexhamPress.com/Christian-Essentials